EMS Public and Community Relations

Edward L. Mund, BA, FF/EMT

Riverside Fire Authority
Centralia, Washington

Emergency Preparedness Coordinator
Lewis County Public Health & Social Services
Chehalis, Washington

EMS Management Series

SERIES EDITOR, *Jeffrey T. Lindsey, PhD, PM, EFO, CFO*
Distance Education Coordinator
for the Fire and Emergency Services Programs
University of Florida
Gainesville, Florida

PEARSON

Boston   Columbus   Indianapolis   New York   San Francisco   Upper Saddle River
Amsterdam   Cape Town   Dubai   London   Madrid   Milan   Munich   Paris   Montreal   Toronto
Delhi   Mexico City   São Paulo   Sydney   Hong Kong   Seoul   Singapore   Taipei   Tokyo

Publisher: Julie Levin Alexander
Publisher's Assistant: Regina Bruno
Editor-in-Chief: Marlene McHugh Pratt
Product Manager: Sladjana Repic
Program Manager: Monica Moosang
Development Editor: Julie M. Vitale, iD8-TripleSSS
Editorial Assistant: Kelly Clark
Director of Marketing: David Gesell
Executive Marketing Manager: Brian Hoehl
Marketing Specialist: Michael Sirinides
Project Management Lead: Cynthia Zonneveld

Project Manager: Julie Boddorf
Full-Service Project Manager: Munesh Kumar, Aptara®, Inc.
Editorial Media Manager: Amy Peltier
Media Project Manager: Ellen Martino
Creative Director: Jayne Conte
Cover Designer: Suzanne Behnke
Cover Image: Shutterstock/B Calkins
Composition: Aptara®, Inc.
Text Font: Times Ten LT Std

Credits and acknowledgments borrowed from other sources and reproduced, with permission, in this textbook appear on the appropriate pages within text.

Copyright © 2015 by Pearson Education, Inc., All rights reserved. Manufactured in the United States of America. This publication is protected by Copyright, and permission should be obtained from the publisher prior to any prohibited reproduction, storage in a retrieval system, or transmission in any form or by any means, electronic, mechanical, photocopying, recording, or likewise. To obtain permission(s) to use material from this work, please submit a written request to Pearson Education, Inc., Permissions Department, One Lake Street, Upper Saddle River, New Jersey 07458, or you may fax your request to 201-236-3290.

Notice: The authors and the publisher of this volume have taken care that the information and technical recommendations contained herein are based on research and expert consultation, and are accurate and compatible with the standards generally accepted at the time of publication. Nevertheless, as new information becomes available, changes in clinical and technical practices become necessary. The reader is advised to carefully consult manufacturers' instructions and information material for all supplies and equipment before use, and to consult with a health care professional as necessary. This advice is especially important when using new supplies or equipment for clinical purposes. The authors and publisher disclaim all responsibility for any liability, loss, injury, or damage incurred as a consequence, directly or indirectly, of the use and application of any of the contents of this volume.

Many of the designations by manufacturers and sellers to distinguish their products are claimed as trademarks. Where those designations appear in this book, and the publisher was aware of a trademark claim, the designations have been printed in initial caps or all caps.

Library of Congress Cataloging-in-Publication Data

Mund, Edward L.
  EMS public information education and relations / Edward L. Mund, BA, FF/EMT & Jeffrey Lindsey, Ph.D., EMT-P, CHS IV, EFO, CFO, St. Petersburg College, St. Petersburg, Florida.
    pages cm
  ISBN-13: 978-0-13-507463-3
  ISBN-10: 0-13-507463-0
  1. Emergency medical personnel—Training of—United States. 2. Emergency medical services—Public relations—United States. I. Lindsey, Jeffrey. II. Title.
  RA645.5.M86 2014
  362.18—dc23   2012033153

ISBN 13: 978-0-13-507463-3
ISBN 10:   0-13-507463-0

Dedication

This book is dedicated to several important individuals. First are my parents, Les and Illma Mund, who inspired and supported my path to becoming a writer, opened my eyes to the value of getting a good education, and instilled in me a passion for giving back to the community. Next is my uncle, Phil Smart, Sr., who is the living embodiment of community volunteerism and one of my most treasured community service role models. Finally, and most of all, to my wife Cindy, thank you for your love, support, being my best friend, and for making the last 30+ years the best of my life.

—ED MUND

I want to dedicate this book to the three best kids in the world—Natasha, Melissa, and Matthew Lindsey—who have always supported me, and in memory of their mother Kandace. I also acknowledge and thank my stepson, Austin Wolfangel, and hope his career ambitions in fire and EMS come true. I also dedicate this to my wife, Sue Wolfangel-Lindsey, with gratitude for her love and understanding. And in gratitude to my parents, Thomas and Janet Lindsey, for always encouraging me in everything I do, I also dedicate this work.

—JEFF LINDSEY

Contents

Preface

Whether your EMS agency is owned and operated by the public, a corporation, a hospital, or a private nonprofit, what you do is a public service. As such, in addition to emergency medicine, one of the important public services you should provide is keeping regulators, community health care and public service partners, the media, and the public informed and educated in general about what your agency does.

This text identifies and offers examples of the informational and educational components that work together to form a comprehensive public relations plan. Capitalizing on successful strategies used in marketing and advertising, it explains the reasons why public information and education are necessary for gaining and holding the public trust. A public information and education tool that EMS managers can personalize to organize and meet their own needs is presented in this book.

Examples are offered throughout this text. They richly illustrate the concepts presented. Information is provided, then demonstrated in use in realistic, EMS-specific situations. The reader will be able to learn a concept, then see it used in a familiar context to help further understanding.

ORGANIZATION OF THIS TEXT

Chapter 1 describes the value to be achieved by any EMS agency that chooses to engage in a robust, ongoing public information and education process. Short-term and long-term gains prove how the time spent reaching various audiences will yield internal and external rewards. Chapter 2 introduces and explains applicable principles of marketing and how they relate to an EMS agency's public relations plan. You will learn how to research and define your own environments and analyze your agency's situation through common marketing analyses methods.

Chapter 3 introduces the Public Information and Education (PIE) Tool, the heart of this text. This four-step tool includes determining your message, identifying the correct audience, crafting the message, and delivering it. The tool can be modified to fit anyone's use. Chapter 4 begins the process of zeroing in on each of the tool's steps in detail, with audience identification. Audience groups are defined, with examples given for each. Chapter 5 offers an outline for identifying your messages by type then categorizing them by audience.

Chapter 6 follows with how to write in terms and concepts that your intended audience will understand. It shows how the same message can be crafted in different ways, depending on who it is being sent to—for example, regulators, employees, the public, and the media. Each of these groups is looking at the message differently. Chapter 6 shows how to speak their languages.

Once your messages are identified and crafted, they have to get from you to their intended audiences. Chapter 7 explores how to deliver messages in writing, in person, through the media, and via the Internet. Chapter 8 is a how-to chapter devoted to the art of writing press releases that will please editors and get published. Clear writing tips and techniques are included with many illustrative examples.

The text concludes in Chapter 9 with a presentation of how to create an information culture in your agency. Teach everyone to look for teachable moments and how to perform the public service of providing information and education with accuracy and professionalism.

The successful EMS manager must be able to clearly communicate his or her desired message no matter to whom that message is going. The more effectively this is done, the better the outcomes will be for that manager's agency in the short term and long term. Mastering the art of public information, education, and public relations is a key component toward a career full of positive outcomes.

FEATURES

Chapter Objectives: Objectives are identified at the beginning of each chapter and outline the material the reader should understand upon completion of the chapter.

Key Terms: Key terms are listed at the beginning of each chapter and are bold upon introduction in the chapter. Each chapter's terms are defined at the end of the chapter, and all terms are included in the comprehensive glossary at the end of the book.

What Would You Do? Case Study: Every chapter starts with an EMS manager tackling some issue related to public information and education that is related to the content of the chapter. How he resolved the issue based on information in the chapter is presented in the **What Would You Do? Reflection** feature at the end of the chapter.

Best Practice: Every chapter includes a real-world example that illustrates information

from the chapter having been used successfully by an EMS agency.

Side Bars: This feature relates interesting information that corresponds very closely to text discussion.

Review Questions: Students are required to draw on the knowledge presented in the chapter to answer the questions.

References: A list of bibliographical references appears at the end of each chapter.

ROAD MAP/HOW TO USE THIS TEXT

This text is designed to be used as a reference and how-to manual for EMS managers seeking to design, implement, and maintain a public relations plan. EMS managers can use the PIE Tool to create templates and reference materials. As information and education needs arise, they can easily and quickly produce the right message for the right audience and ensure its delivery.

TEACHING AND LEARNING RESOURCES

For information on instructor resources, including PowerPoint presentations and assessment tools, please contact your Brady sales representative.

ACKNOWLEDGMENTS

To my co-author, Jeff Lindsey, who was a great mentor, tutor, partner, and constant source of information, inspiration, and clarification whenever I needed it.

To the professionals at Brady who shepherded us and this project from inception through completion with good humor and sound principles.

To the reviewers for their invaluable feedback and their dedication to the EMS profession.

To all the teachers, professors, and role models throughout my life who inspire and improve my ability to craft words on a page.

—ED MUND

To my co-author, Ed Mund, who was great to work with and provided an excellent perspective on this topic.

To the wonderful staff at Brady: Marlene Pratt and Monica Moosang.

To our developmental editor, Julie Vitale.

To all the reviewers for their feedback and encouragement to make this a great text!

To all those who read this text, thanks for taking the time. It is my desire that your efforts make an impact in the EMS profession for the betterment of all.

—JEFF LINDSEY

We would also like to thank the following reviewers for their feedback:

Diane Flint
Program Director
University of Maryland, Baltimore County
Dept. of Emergency Health Services, EHS
Undergraduate Management
Baltimore, MD

Travis Fox, EMT-P
Paramedic Clinical Coordinator
University of Antelope Valley
Paramedic Program
Lancaster, CA

David Harrington
Battalion Chief, City of Oak Ridge Fire Department
Adjunct Instructor, Roane State Community College
Knoxville, TN

Steve Lynn
Firefighter, Paramedic, Adjunct Instructor
Southwestern Illinois College
Highland, IL

Keith Monosky, PhD, MPM, EMT-P
Associate Professor
Department of Nutrition, Exercise, and Health Sciences & Director of the EMS Paramedicine Program
Central Washington University
Ellensburg, WA

Douglas Rohn, Lieutenant
Madison Fire Department
Madison, WI

Mike Taigman
Assistant Professor
UMBC Department of Emergency Health Services
San Diego, CA

Michael Vastano, NREMT-P
EMT Program Director
Education and Training Department
Captain James A.
Lovell Federal Health Care Center

About the Authors

EDWARD L. MUND, BA, FF/EMT

Edward L. Mund, BA, FF/EMT, has enjoyed a long career in the journalism, advertising, and marketing industries, along with a simultaneous career in emergency medicine and the fire service. This has left him with a wide range of professional experiences to draw from for co-authoring this textbook.

In 1978 Ed graduated with a B.A. in Journalism from Western Washington University in Bellingham, Washington. For the next 10 years he worked in, and later managed, the pre-press operations producing dozens of newspapers in downtown Seattle, Washington.

From 1988 to 2009, he was the business manager and copywriter for an ad agency in Olympia, Washington, where he wrote informational and promotional materials for hundreds of private, commercial, nonprofit, and governmental clients.

Ed began his fire and EMS career in 1989 with East Olympia Fire District 6 in Thurston County, Washington, where he attained the rank of Captain and served as EMS Officer for 11 years. He was a long-time EMS instructor in the two-tiered, countywide EMS system. He currently serves with Riverside Fire Authority, a fire-based ALS agency in Centralia, Washington.

Ed represents the Washington State Fire Fighters' Association on the Washington State Governor's EMS and Trauma Care Steering Committee and its Prehospital Technical Advisory Committee. He is a past board member and former Secretary/Treasurer of the Washington State Fire Fighters' Association and serves as its EMS Liaison and Media Relations contact. He is a member of the National Volunteer Fire Council and its EMS/Rescue Section, and the National Association of EMTs. He also serves on the Patient Advisory Council for two Providence Health & Services hospitals in Washington.

In addition to co-authoring this text, he also authored the Brady *Foundations of EMS Systems* textbook and was the editor of two published history books. Ed owns and operates his own fire and EMS training company and serves as a lecturer, content author, subject matter expert, and photographer for national EMS and fire service training providers. He has been published in multiple print and online trade publications and regularly contributes articles and photos to *EMS World* magazine.

JEFFREY T. LINDSEY, PH.D., PM, EFO, CFO

Dr. Jeffrey Lindsey has served in a variety of roles in the fire and EMS arena for the past 30 years. He has held positions of firefighter, paramedic, dispatcher, educator, coordinator, deputy chief, and chief. He started his career in Carlisle, Pennsylvania, as a volunteer firefighter/EMT. In 1985 Dr. Lindsey pioneered the first advanced life support service in Cumberland County, Pennsylvania. He is retired as the Fire/EMS Chief for Estero Fire Rescue, where he served as the South Division Incident Commander during major events. He was also part of the Area Command for Lee County EOC. Currently he is the Distance Education Coordinator for the Fire and Emergency Services Programs at the University of Florida.

He has served as an inaugural member on the National EMS Advisory Council, representing fire-based EMS, and is a past member of the State of Florida EMS Advisory Council, where he served as the firefighter/paramedic representative. He currently serves as representative to the Fire and Emergency Services Higher Education EMS degree committee. He has been active in the IAFC, serving as liaison to ACEP and attending various meetings representing fire-based EMS, and as the inaugural chair of the Community Paramedic committee, and he is an associate member of the Prehospital Research Forum.

He was a monthly columnist on product reviews for 3 years for *The Journal of Emergency Medical Services (JEMS)*, a national EMS journal. He is a columnist for Firerehab.com and has authored numerous fire and EMS texts for Brady/Pearson. He is currently the Chief Learning Officer for the Health and Safety Institute, which produces *24-7 EMS* and *24-7 Fire* videos. He also was an EMS professor for St. Petersburg College (Florida).

Dr. Lindsey has been involved in a number of large events and has served within the incident command system at the upper level, including during a number of wildland fires and Hurricane Charley. He has also been involved in the preparations for a number of other hurricanes and tropical storms.

He holds an associate's degree in paramedicine from Harrisburg Area Community College, a bachelor's degree in Fire and Safety from the University of Cincinnati, a master's degree in Instructional Technology from the University of South Florida, and a Ph.D. in Instructional Technology/Adult Education from the University of South Florida.

In addition, Dr. Lindsey has completed the Executive Fire Officer Program at the National Fire Academy. He has designed and developed various courses in fire and EMS. Dr. Lindsey is accredited with the Chief Fire Officer Designation. He also is a certified Fire Officer II, Fire Instructor III, and paramedic in the state of Florida; holds a paramedic certificate for the state of Pennsylvania; and is a certified instructor in these and a variety of other courses.

Dr. Lindsey has an innate interest in alternative health. He is a certified nutritional counselor, a master herbalist, and a holistic health practitioner.

About FESHE

FESHE (Fire and Emergency Services Higher Education) is a dedicated group of individuals from around the country. It is hosted by the United States Fire Administration through the National Fire Academy. The mission of this group is to develop a uniform model curriculum for associates, bachelor, and masters degree. In December 2006 a group of EMS educators convened as the inaugural EMS committee for FESHE. The mission was to develop a model curriculum in EMS management at the bachelor level. It was the consensus of the leaders across the country that the committee focus on the management issues of EMS. The clinical portion of the industry is addressed through the National EMS Education Standards and is mainly focused at the associate's level.

This text is written to meet the needs of the national model curriculum for EMS management at the bachelor's level. The EMS management curriculum includes six core courses and seven elective courses. Following are titles in Brady's *EMS Management Series*, designed to meet the FESHE curriculum.

CORE

- Foundations of EMS Systems
- Management of EMS
- EMS Community Risk Reduction
- EMS Quality Management and Research
- Legal, Political and Regulatory Environment in EMS
- EMS Safety and Risk Management

ELECTIVE

- Management of Ambulance Services
- Foundations for the Practice of EMS Education
- EMS Special Operations
- EMS Public Information and Community Relations
- EMS Communications and Information Technology
- EMS Finance
- Analytical Approaches to EMS

Value of Public Information, Education, and Relations

1 CHAPTER

Objectives

After reading this chapter, the student should be able to:

1.1 Define the meanings and importance of public information, education, and public relations.
1.2 Describe the various audiences to keep informed.
1.3 Identify the qualities of a successful public information officer.

Overview

This title identifies and offers examples of the informational and educational components that work together to form a comprehensive public relations plan. Capitalizing on successful strategies used in marketing and advertising, it explains the reasons why public information and education are necessary for gaining and holding the public trust.

Key Terms

partners
public education
public information

public relations
public service
   announcements
   (PSAs)

stakeholders
targeted audiences

WHAT WOULD YOU DO?

Public relations are part of many other job assignments. *Source: Steve Gorton/Dorling Kindersley.*

Les Phillips has just been promoted to EMS Division Chief of the Cooks Hill Fire Department (CHFD). First hired as a paramedic/firefighter 20 years ago, he was promoted through the ranks of lieutenant to captain and now division chief in charge of emergency medical services (EMS) at CHFD. His new job description includes taking care of public relations and being the first point of contact for any media inquiries related to CHFD EMS operations or incidents.

Twenty years in the streets providing patient care, crew leadership, and ongoing training have given Les ample opportunities to learn how to communicate in the here and now. But this new job will require that he learn more about CHFD than he ever knew, learn how to interact with the media, and expand his skills to become an advocate for CHFD to any and all who need to be reached.

Questions

1. What exactly are public information, public education, and public relations?
2. Who are the multiple audiences Les needs to identify and reach?
3. Where can Les turn to learn what he needs to know about CHFD?

■ INTRODUCTION

Successful EMS chiefs understand the need to communicate in a variety of ways with a number of different audiences. Among those audiences are **stakeholders** and **partners**. Stakeholders affect how the EMS agency operates. Stakeholders can include officials who control the agency's budget and rule makers who define the parameters of patient care that agency responders can do in the field. They must be kept informed of the agency's goals, needs, accomplishments, and challenges. Partners are outside interests such as law enforcement, public works, and public health. They share a common interest in public service, help the agency do its job, and must be continually informed and educated about the agency's operations, new programs, quality assurance (QA) and quality improvement (QI) issues pertaining to joint operations, and goals to be mutually achieved.

The successful EMS chief must be able to identify public groups such as the elderly or parents with bicycle-riding children or neighborhood associations, prepare messages that are meaningful to both the agency and groups, and ensure these messages reach their intended recipients.

Groups to be communicated with are identified in a number of ways. In addition to the public, EMS chiefs will also need to communicate with groups who hold regulatory and financial authority over the agency, groups that work with the agency to help it serve the public, members of the press, and their own personnel.

Maintaining constant and consistent lines of communication with all of these groups reaps benefits for the agency's finances, operations, and reputation. You want people with regulatory and fiscal control over your operations to have an informed and positive view of your agency. Other agencies with whom you work on behalf of the citizens in your service area will help your agency do its job when they know exactly what you do and what you expect of them. Positive relations with the public and the press reaps dividends at election time for public agencies, and any time a question, concern, or complaint arises.

You are encouraged to adapt and apply the information in this chapter to your specific situation. As you read the examples, use your own points of reference to put them in proper context for your agency. Whether your budget comes from a city council, county commission, board of directors, or some other source, the principles of keeping them informed and educated about your operations remain the same. Likewise, improving your on-scene interactions with law enforcement are just as important regardless of whether you work with city police, a county sheriff's department, state police, or a combination of multiple agencies.

Why spend time on public information, education, and relations in the first place? It is a cumbersome chore to most, and it doesn't show the same immediate, direct positive effect that, say, restocking the medical bag does. This chapter will introduce you to the short- and long-term positive outcomes that can be gained by learning who to talk to and being the master of your own information.

DEFINITIONS AND DIFFERENTIATION

Most people use the terms **public information**, **public education**, and **public relations** interchangeably. To a certain extent they are correct in that each of these terms involves getting a message of some type to someone you want to receive it. Successfully getting someone to hear your message depends on your ability to craft the message in words they understand and to send the message via a conduit likely to reach the recipients. Teaching the general public to call 9-1-1 at the onset of chest pain is one type of message; we'll use it for an example of how to define and differentiate public information, education, and relations.

PUBLIC INFORMATION

The goal of a public information effort is to make a general or specific audience aware of the existence of something. Deep understanding by your audience is not required—only the knowledge that the item or process being discussed is available.

Day after day you hear EMS crews coming back from "chest pain" calls and saying "If only they had called sooner." By talking to the crews, you learn that many of the patients have bad outcomes simply because they waited too long to call 9-1-1 for help when they first started feeling unwell. Maybe they were in denial, maybe they didn't think of calling, or maybe they were afraid to call because they had no money. The reasons why they don't call are not as important as getting them to use the phone and dial 9-1-1.

A general public information campaign would simply promote calling 9-1-1 when you first start feeling pain in your chest. In a general information campaign like this, brevity of message and widespread distribution are the keys to success.

Through **public service announcements (PSAs)**, patients learn what to do and when. Their loved ones also hear the message. Everybody learns to call 9-1-1 when the pain starts, and to make the call themselves or make it for the patient. In a brief PSA there's no time, or need, to delve into the typical and atypical signs and symptoms. You do not explain why. You want only to deliver a brief, easily remembered punch to the audience, such as "Chest pain? Call 9-1-1 for help immediately."

Think of public information as making the public more knowledgeable about the subject at hand. In our example, you want them to know to call 9-1-1 when chest pain starts. Remembering this will prompt a cascade of thoughts that can lead up to doing the right thing for their health.

Chest pain = 9-1-1 now

9-1-1 = paramedics now

Paramedics = making it to the hospital alive

Better call 9-1-1 NOW!

Information gives them the "what." The next step is public education aimed at helping the public further understand why calling 9-1-1 is a good idea.

PUBLIC EDUCATION

Public education is the process of informing a general or specific audience of the existence of something, along with details such as how, why, when, where, and why it matters to them. Public education can be a stand-alone process, incorporating information along with education. Or it can be used as a follow-up, using familiar references from a previous public information campaign, then adding educational components to achieve the intended goals.

Follow-up with a public education process could be used to extend and increase the effectiveness of the "Chest Pain = 9-1-1" public information campaign. A well-crafted public education campaign will reach its **targeted audiences**, the people who can benefit the most from the message. You want to speak directly to your audience's questions, fears, and misconceptions; give them reasons to want to do what you suggest; and increase their knowledge about your agency's EMS operations.

With years of experience in EMS, you already know who your targeted audiences are: adults in their prime risk years for heart attacks, as well as the people around them, such as spouses and children, who can influence their decisions.

Next, you need to know why people are not calling so you can teach them how their reasons are negatively impacting their outcomes. In interviewing your EMS crews, you discover the most common reasons they recall for delays in dialing 9-1-1 are denial, fear of learning the truth, and cost.

You pull together facts, figures, and statistics to prove how immediately calling 9-1-1 as an early intervention improves outcomes. Include details on how the EMS system works and what the EMS responders can do in someone's home. Present this information to overcome denial and fear by showing how the patient has his or her best chance of survival if the condition is indeed a heart attack. If it is not a heart attack, it could be something leading to one, and that could be prevented. Perhaps another, less serious condition could be identified and resolved.

To overcome fear of a large bill, present information on how calling 9-1-1, the paramedic response, and transport to the hospital are paid for. If your 9-1-1 center, response, and transport are prepaid through taxes or other means, be sure to include these facts. If local agencies provide financial assistance for services to the underinsured and uninsured, include details and contact information. Show people when the financial risk is absent or manageable and no reason to refrain from calling for help.

Figure 1.1 ▪ Strategically placing public information in central locations, such as waiting area of offices, is important for distribution of materials to the public. *Courtesy of Jeffrey T. Lindsey, Ph.D.*

Once you have all this information bundled and drafted, you have multiple ways to reach the public. The first and obvious choice is through the mass media, which can be in the form of PSAs, interview-based news items, press releases, and guest columns.

A second choice is to place *Call 9-1-1* brochures in hospital emergency departments, urgent care centers, clinics, physician's offices, senior centers, and other places your **target audiences** patronize. (See Figure 1.1.)

A third option is to give your EMS street crews a supply of your *Call 9-1-1* brochures for their rigs. Inform them of the reasons for creating the brochures, the research and content that have gone into them, and how and when to distribute them. As the crews run calls and identify addresses with potential future cardiac risks, they can leave a brochure and

answer any questions the patient or family member may have.

Now that you have reached your audiences, they can answer the "Why do this?" "What's in it for me?" and "How does my EMS system work?" questions. Educated people experiencing chest pain are more likely to call 9-1-1 immediately because their fears and objections have already been addressed and overcome.

PUBLIC RELATIONS

Public relations is a catchall term used to describe some type of public outreach. In reality, however, public relations is the goal of its two key strategies: public information and public education. The Public Relations Society of America (PRSA) has adopted the following definition of public relations: "Public relations helps an organization and its publics adapt mutually to each other."

Good public relations is the sum total of effective public information and education efforts. In the process, your agency identifies and adapts its operations to better inform, educate, and serve its stakeholders, partners, and public audiences. Through your efforts, these groups have gained a better understanding of how their EMS agency operates and how to best serve or use the agency's services on their own behalf. Mutual adaptation is achieved when attitudes and behavior are changed for the better.

In the Call 9-1-1 information campaign, the agency responded to the public's failure to call for help by informing and reminding the targeted audiences why calling 9-1-1 is important. The campaign can be deemed successful when audiences adapt by calling for help.

The Call 9-1-1 education campaign prompted the agency to research and adapt its messaging to learn why people did not call on time and to prepare outreach that explained the benefits while allaying known fears. Again, in a successful campaign, the time between onset of chest pain and calling 9-1-1 will decrease as targeted audiences adapt their attitudes and behavior to embrace the EMS agency's assistance.

EMS crews feel good when they do something preventive. The public feels good that the local EMS agency cares about them and that their fears and questions are resolved. The goal of good public relations has been achieved on this particular issue through the effective use of public information and education. As the PRSA notes in its definition, through these interactions the organization and its public have adapted mutually to each other.

The fire service has used public relations techniques successfully with smoke detectors and detector battery programs. Both fire and EMS services have also used children's car seats and bicycle helmet programs to enhance public relations in their jurisdictions.

■ MULTIPLE AUDIENCES

Your agency impacts a large number of individuals, groups, organizations, and agencies. As a result, these audiences are interested in your agency, some more so than others. These various audiences can be divided into the following five categories: stakeholders, partners, the public, employees, and the press. Key players in these audience categories impact your service. Knowing more about who they are and what they do is important for maintaining good public relations with them all.

STAKEHOLDERS

Stakeholders have the power to control how your agency operates through legislation, funding, rules, and regulations. Stakeholder groups have the authority over how the agency functions as a whole, how much money it has to spend, what areas it can serve, how the agency and individual members are licensed, and who leads the department.

Publicly owned agencies have elected or appointed officials who oversee how public tax money is spent. Examples are city councils, county commissions, or boards or commissions elected or appointed to oversee a specific agency. These officials are stakeholders in that they control how an entity is funded. They also often have the authority to hire and fire the chief.

Emergency medical technicians (EMTs) and paramedics are trained in programs certified by the state and/or local governing councils. Each EMT and paramedic must successfully complete initial and ongoing training to become and remain licensed or certified to perform in those jobs. The training, certification, and licensing agency is a stakeholder because it has the authority to say who can do patient care and at what level of training.

State lawmakers and local councils also serve as stakeholders in that they set in law the scope of practice for EMTs and paramedics. These stakeholders define the rules that specify what skills can be performed; what medicines, equipment, and procedures can be used on patients; and who is authorized to work on EMS units.

State and local regulatory stakeholders have a third function in the authority to investigate reported breaches of the rules. They have the option to discipline, suspend, and revoke the licenses of agencies and individual providers.

A fourth state and local stakeholder function is as the conduit to the public for laws passed by the state legislature. Legislation passed and signed by the governor that impacts or proscribes how EMS agencies operate is passed to state and local regulatory agencies for implementation. Agencies write rules that become the standards all EMS agencies must follow in order to comply with the new law.

An EMS agency may contract with a local emergency medicine physician to oversee its emergency medical operations as the agency's medical program director (MPD). As a stakeholder, the MPD may authorize scope of practice and equipment that exceeds what the state or local regulatory agencies require. He or she also has the authority to approve the credentials of any EMS provider, working in his or her agency, as well as to initiate investigations and disciplinary actions against these EMS personnel.

Part of public relations efforts must be aimed at keeping all stakeholders informed and educated about how the agency operates and what impact their decisions make on your operations for better or worse. The more regulators know, the more easily they can be persuaded to see the positive impacts as well as the negative consequences of any actions or pending requests.

With a good relationship between the agency and the MPD, the MPD can also be considered in the next audience category as a partner, lending expertise to help personnel excel in patient care. With a great relationship, the MPD spends more time and effort as your partner than as a stakeholder.

PARTNERS

Simply put, partners help your agency do its job, day in and day out. One key partner is the public safety access point (PSAP) (see Figure 1.2) or, as it's more traditionally called, the dispatch center. Without the PSAP to answer 9-1-1 calls for help, dispatch units, be a resource for units in the field, and coordinate other agencies on the same incident, EMS responders would never get out of the station.

Law enforcement is a second important strategic partner for EMS agencies. Depending on the geographic area served, an EMS agency may work with a single law enforcement agency, or multiple agencies, including local police, the county sheriff's department, state police, federal agencies, and tribal police. Since all law enforcement agencies, though similar in mission, have their own ways of doing things, it is important to know about them before running into each other on scene.

Some EMS responders, particularly in fire-based agencies, do not routinely transport patients. Local and national privately owned ambulance companies are contracted to provide fee-for-service patient transportation. EMS agency paramedics and EMTs respond to 9-1-1 calls, assess and stabilize the patients, then transfer care to the third-party vendor for transport to the hospital. EMS personnel with different agencies may be trained and licensed at the same level by the same state and local agencies and may practice under the same MPD for continuity of care.

FIGURE 1.2 ■ A key stakeholder is the PSAP.

Local hospitals and urgent care centers that accept transported 9-1-1 patients are partners, even if the EMS agency is not transporting. Patient care in the field, destination selection, and other factors that improve patient outcomes are driven by the capacity, capabilities, and requirements of these receiving facilities.

As with stakeholders, the more you and your partners know about how each other operates, the better the interactions will be with your respective personnel, both in the field and in planning operations. An effective educational strategy is to let each partner experience the other partner's world. EMS responders should spend time in the dispatch center to see firsthand what that job is and how it is done. Dispatchers should do ride-alongs with EMS responders to see what happens on the other end of their radio traffic.

Get permission to have law enforcement and EMS responders do ride-alongs with each other. Even though EMS and law enforcement

resources are often on the same scene at the same time, they have different priorities and jobs to do. Ride-along programs let both sides take a new look at the next scene from their partner's perspective as well as their own. Allow dispatchers, law enforcement, and other partners to ride along with EMS responders.

Have EMS responders spend time in a destination hospital emergency department, especially if they are working in a nontransport agency that never sees the outcome of its patient care firsthand. The responders may be just observers, or they may actively participate in further patient care, depending on the discretion of the hospital administration. Hospital emergency department personnel should participate in field ride-alongs to learn more about the circumstances surrounding how patients are accessed, treated, and transported. This will give them a better understanding of the challenges faced doing patient care up to the point where the patient arrives at the hospital.

PUBLIC

Members of the public can be looked at in their entirety, and as various special-interest groups. The overall public for an EMS agency is anyone in its service area, whether the individuals live there, work there, come into the area for some other reason, or are just passing through.

After this, the public can be divided into as many separate groups as there are collections of people, such as neighborhood associations, schools, and service organizations.

Neighborhood associations are comprised of people who care about their little corner of the world and are concerned about how well and quickly their local EMS responders can serve them. High schools, middle schools, and elementary schools have their own parent/teacher/student associations; outreach to them covers the school population as well as a multitude of neighborhoods. Hobbyists, scouts, and commercial club and community service organization members are predisposed to community service and eager to learn what they can about their local agency and how they can help.

EMPLOYEES

It is not possible to personally interact with all the stakeholders, partners, and public groups in and around your agency's service area. But you can still have a tremendous impact on them all if you train your personnel to engage in public information and public education.

Personnel participation starts in the streets, answering questions from patients, their family members, and the general public. Personnel don't have to wait to be asked, either. An example would be where the closest paramedic unit took 25 minutes to respond to a motor vehicle crash in a remote corner of its service area. Meanwhile, volunteer EMTs from a closer station were on scene in less than 5 minutes, had extricated the patients, and had initiated good patient care. At the end of the call, that is an opportunity to tell witnesses, participants, and bystanders about how the volunteers save time, money, and, last but not least, lives. Personnel trained to recognize these teachable moments and who have the facts available to present when the time is right turned the crash in this example into a great public relations event and recruiting opportunity for the department.

Personnel can also attend some community events and meetings on behalf of the department. Staging a staffed unit at school events, a neighborhood garage sale, health fairs, and other community gatherings gives the public more opportunities to see and learn about the department.

PRESS

The press is a unique audience. Reporters consider their participation in world events from the third-person perspective. That means they write news as an observer telling the story, rather than as a participant in the story. Thus, you should treat the press as its own entity, separate from your other audiences. (See Figure 1.3.) In some ways, the press is a partner, helping you reach your audiences. In other ways, it can almost take on the role of a stakeholder if its investigations and reporting cause changes to your agency. Which audience your local press fits into depends in large part on how well you conduct your outreach to them.

Depending on the location, an EMS agency may have to work with local, regional, state, national, and even international press outlets. Local daily and weekly newspapers and larger daily newspapers from neighboring metropolitan areas are typical print media outlets. Local and regional radio and television stations are common electronic media outlets. With cable and satellite television operators

FIGURE 1.3 ■ It is critical to reach out to the local media to establish rapport and make them a stakeholder. *Source: Dorling Kindersley.*

extending their reach throughout the United States, more communities have local access television channels to provide programming within that community. Studios are available for scheduled public-interest programming and for groups wishing to create public-service programs.

Outreach to the Press

EMS managers should make the rounds of the editors and reporters who cover the fire and EMS beat in their area. In reaching out to them, you can let them know who to contact at the agency. You also get to know each one individually to learn what they know about the agency, what agendas they may have, and what kind of information they prefer to publish. This helps you package information for them that fills in the gaps in their knowledge base, provides information of interest to their readers or listeners, and stands a better chance of being published or incorporated into a news story.

Side Bar

The Public Information Officer (PIO) has a number of responsibilities. In order to fulfill these duties and responsibilities of the PIO you need to have the following knowledge base:

- Demonstrate effective writing skills for internal and external communication
- Maintain a professional appearance at all times
- Utilize time management skills
- Know the characteristics and processes of the media in the community
- Utilize various methods for information gathering
- Develop messages in accordance with the event or incident
- Disseminate and monitor information
- Use information technology, including social media
- Know all internal and external customers.

Establish community relationships and know the resources available in the community

Have a working knowledge of the incident management system

Be part of the organizational emergency and nonemergency functions

Identify and respond to proactive message opportunities

Prepare and manage a budget

Perform both internal and external marketing for the organization

Know and follow applicable public information laws, standards, and policies

Pique the media's interest with human interest stories about patients (with permission from the patients, of course), personnel honors, what personnel do when not at the station, and background about new procedures, vehicles, or equipment. Conduct ride-along programs with senior personnel you've coached to work with the press. Facilitate similar programs with your partners so the reporter can follow every step of an emergency medical event from the PSAP to the patient's side, then to the hospital, and ultimately to discharge.

The goodwill developed with that media outlet and the interest from the public at large will pay huge dividends for the agency the next time any kind of controversy comes up. People who already have a favorable opinion of the agency will be more objective about any charges against it.

As you reach out to the press, be careful not to appear as though you are favoring one publication over another, or one station over another. All your efforts to curry favor with a reporter or editor you like to work with will be wasted if other reporters and editors feel cheated. Not only might you lose any goodwill you had with the other media, but you also

might tempt the other to start looking for reasons not to like you and your agency and then publish some slanted results.

Responding to the Press

On the other side of the press coin, making yourself available to the press helps ensure that you are contacted by them first for information and comments, which in turn will help you manage the message and public face of the department's EMS operations.

Contact from the press is a test of your credibility. Any new hire may be asked about things the reporter already knows just to see how good a source he or she will be. Reporters want to know if their sources are truthful, knowledgeable, and truly empowered to speak for your agency. If any of those attributes are absent, the reporter will move on to another source. Then you will have a more difficult time working with him or her and possibly other reporters.

Responding to reporters working on fast-moving or breaking stories at deadline will be the strongest test of the relationship you have formed. Above all else, be honest. If you don't know the answer, be honest and say so, along with your best estimate of when you will have the information. If you do know, but are not at liberty to divulge the information, say so. Don't say you don't know when you really do; say you're sorry, but that information cannot be released. If you know when it will be cleared, say so. Of course, if you do know the answer and can reveal it, by all means do so.

Partnering with the Press

With appropriate and fearless outreach and responsiveness, you are telling the press that you want to work with them. Building rapport early will give the press the sense that you are a partner they can access and trust to help them do their jobs.

Reporters always want more information than what is published or read on the air. This helps them more fully understand the story, and it lets the reporter and editor decide which facts are the most salient to the story and interesting to the readers. As the expert on EMS operations in your agency, you are the press's in-house partner at your agency. Make as much background information available to them as you can.

One way to quench the press's never-ending thirst for information is to spend hours on end talking with reporters as they call with questions. A better way is to build a resource library for the media. Create a notebook full of what reporters refer to as boilerplate—facts and details about your EMS operations—and give a copy to every reporter and editor with whom you have contact. Include facts about the budget, service area, number of personnel, call volume, vehicles, equipment, and anything else that routinely comes up in stories.

Take this information and post it on your agency's website, too, so any reporters at any hour have immediate access to all information right at their fingertips. As new queries or information come in, add them to the website as well. Post to the site for archival access every press release you write.

When you extend yourself to the local press, answer their questions truthfully and promptly, and make it easy for them to get information they need, you have converted what is typically an adversarial relationship into a true public information partnership.

■ BE THE EXPERT

As the voice of and for your EMS agency, you must be perceived as the expert about all aspects of how your agency provides EMS services. The National Fire Protection Association (NFPA) provides an excellent structure to follow.

DEFINE THE POSITION

NFPA 1035: Standard for Professional Qualifications for Public Fire and Life Safety Educator from the National Fire Protection Association provides many elements of a job definition and qualifications that you can use in your EMS position. Even though the topics may differ for fire and EMS, the basic qualifications and principles of public outreach are common. If you follow the requisite knowledge and skills suggestions in the NFPA standard, you will become an expert in your agency as well as your chosen profession.

FACTS AND FIGURES

Become an encyclopedia full of information, facts, and figures about your agency's EMS operations, including the common benchmarks such as call volume, budget, and staffing. Dig deeper, too, to find the trivia tidbits that everyone finds so interesting. The number of oxygen masks used in a year, the number of miles driven, gallons of fuel burned, price of a new medic unit, cost of its contents—all these add dimension and interest to the agency's public image.

It is easier to garner support at special election times, or during budget negotiations, when the public and other stakeholders are already aware of the scope and challenges of running your EMS operations. You can find much of this information in your agency's annual report if it produces one. Public agencies' budgets are public record and easy to examine. Get acquainted with your agency's purchasing manager for numbers of items used and costs. Catalog these facts and figures where they can be easily retrieved. Knowing them makes you a more thorough expert on your system. Being able to use them in conversation or written communications demonstrates your expertise and raises your credibility.

LOCAL SYSTEM DESIGNS

The EMS industry is well known for having multiple models for delivering emergency medical services to communities. Fire-based, hospital-based, all-advanced life support (ALS), two-tiered, paid, volunteer, combination, public, private—these are just some of the system designs in use today.

Become an expert on your agency's system design, along with the reasons for its initial selection and ongoing use. But that's only part of the picture. For every argument for one model, you'll find equally passionate arguments against it. That is why it is important to become not just an expert in the how's and why's of your own system, but also to become knowledgeable of other system designs. (See Figure 1.4.)

Stakeholders, partners, the public, and the press may all question you about why your EMS services are delivered in the chosen manner. With their limited expertise, they may assert that another way is better and question why your agency is not using it. You need an in-depth knowledge of the various systems, along with the pros and cons of each, in order to accurately compare, answer questions, and, if necessary, defend your system's design.

REGIONAL AND STATE INTERACTIONS

No EMS agency is an island unto itself. Multiple layers of government stakeholders impact the agency in many ways, including requirements for what equipment is carried on the units, training and licensing of personnel, scope of practice, and service area. These stakeholders may also be sources of significant nonlocal funding.

Learn where every rule, every regulation, and every law originates. Learn how rules and regulations that affect your agency are created from law, and how you and your personnel can participate in that process. Learn the sources of the funding you receive from regional and state stakeholders, how it is distributed, and how to participate in that process. At the same time you are protecting your own interests, you are creating opportunities to inform and educate these stakeholder groups about how their actions affect your operations.

FIGURE 1.4   ■   There are many models of EMS systems.

LINES OF AUTHORITY

To effectively speak for and represent the EMS operations in your agency, you must have a clear understanding of your freedoms and limitations. You need to establish parameters of performance and authority with your immediate superior, and higher up if need be, in your agency. You must be certain about what you can and cannot say or do when reporters are calling about an incident, or you are testifying before a stakeholder group, or a neighborhood association is asking for participation in a community event.

Looking down the chain of command, you must also be clear with your staff. They need to know what they are allowed to do or say, and to what they may commit their unit. Depending on your comfort level, they may be allowed to commit the agency or their unit to a specific event while on or off duty. If not, they need to know just where to draw the line on requests for information or public participation.

■ BENEFITS GAINED FROM TIME INVESTED

Your duty day is already overflowing with shift scheduling, personnel matters, report reviews, meetings, planning, and so on. Where is the value of public information, education, and relations to the organization, and is it worth taking time away from some other figurative fire you always have smoldering on your desk?

The value of public relations is that by making a small investment up front, you begin an escalating chain of events that results in making tomorrow a better day for your agency as it interacts with all of its various audiences. A knowledgeable public is supportive of the agency and knows to call 9-1-1 in time for your crews to preserve a life.

Stakeholders with whom you have established a relationship of trust and openness will be more likely to consult with you as they consider regulatory or financial actions. When they are more aware of the downstream effects of their actions, they can more carefully consider consequences as well as advantages of proposed actions.

Mutual understanding among partners working together in the field yield smoother, more efficient operations, and interpersonal interactions. These partners are also likely to work together to preplan mutual events and guidelines for mutual response, both of which result in better operational performance.

Establishing good rapport with the press increases the likelihood that interactions with

Best Practices

Lee County (Florida) EMS personnel have taken Public Information, Education, and Relations (PIER) services so seriously that they have based their program based on the state EMS plan and the national PIER program. It is considered a core component of their EMS service. The goal of the program is to "provide up-to-date information to the citizens and visitors of Lee County, so they may be aware of their EMS system and have access to information and education to enhance their daily living." The following are several of the programs in Lee County's PIER program:

• Heartsaver First Aid, CPR, and Automated External Defibrillation (AED) Training
• Child Passenger Safety Seat Inspections
• Speakers Bureau
• Public Access Defibrillation (PAD)
• Ambulance Tour

You can find contact information on Lee County's PIER program at www.lee-ems.com.

them will be cordial rather than adversarial. Personnel who are kept "in the know," and offered opportunities to interact with their agency's audiences in a setting that is not focused on patient care, take more pride and ownership in their agency. Such personnel are more likely to resolve issues at lower levels, overlook unintentional errors, and become vested in community outreach efforts.

It is worth spending time on public relations, even when you are busy with pressing issues, because doing so can prevent many problems from ever occurring. Anything you do that increases an audience's knowledge and support for your agency lessens the chances of having an adverse experience with that audience. Allies give their allies the benefit of the doubt. Little issues are easier to shrug off. Even when a problem does arise, resolution is faster and easier between two allies than between two adversaries.

It is true that information is power, so sharing information and educating everyone who uses and impacts your agency is the quickest path to getting buy-in from them, whether it's something as simple as when to call 9-1-1 or as complex as explaining the annual operations budget. In this respect, your information empowers you to enable others to help you achieve your goals of managing EMS operations and serving the public.

SHORT-TERM GAINS

Short-term gains can range in time from a few minutes to a few months. Ideally, distributing information for short-term gains is either a reminder about or a logical extension of information that the targeted audience already knows from a larger, long-term campaign already in place.

For example, perhaps it is time for a popular annual health fair hosted by your department for the past 50 years. (See Figure 1.5.) The long-term information and educational campaign has been 50 years in the making.

FIGURE 1.5 ■ Health fairs are a great way to reach out to the public.

All you need to do now is remind the public that the health fair is drawing near and provide dates, times, and location. You would also include enough information to remind veteran attendees how much fun it was last year. At the same time, these details introduce the event and generate interest among newcomers to your community.

On the other hand, the unpredictability of EMS also requires you to be fast on your feet in order to react to emergency or unplanned events. You have to be able to quickly gather and present information in response to unanticipated queries. You also need to have others in your organization aligned with your efforts.

Short-Term Gains Within Your Organization

Sharing information helps build trust among you, your personnel, and your peers. Bringing these people into the information loop tells them you respect and trust them enough not to be threatened by this sharing. Knowing the rationale behind shift schedules or partner trades makes this kind of change easier for your staff to accept and even embrace. Knowing why you're asking them to participate in a community event on their day off sends them to the event with a better attitude and your public relations goals in mind.

Providing internal information and education is a sure method for controlling rumors. As already noted, your personnel group is one of your audiences, and information is power. Rumors start in the absence of good information. As the only one talking, the rumor monger is in a position of power. He or she may not be exercising that power with the best interests of the department and your programs in mind but, rather, may be pursuing self-interests instead.

The best solution to rumors is not to let them start. An open and sharing information culture within the organization offers little fertile ground for rumors to grow. When they

do, immediate distribution of facts robs self-interested parties of their power, and you regain control of the issue and organization.

Short-Term Gains Outside Your Organization

Most of what the people in your community know about EMS comes from movies and television shows. Stakeholders have been "educated" by the entertainment industry to believe that your response time is under 2 minutes, most heart attack victims live, and major trauma patients go from injury to surgery to recovery within the time limits of a 60-minute prime-time drama. Failing to live up to their perception of reality is a daily and ongoing challenge.

Every call every day provides an opportunity to shine a little light on the reality outside a film or television studio. EMS providers are excellent communicators. Give your staff the informational tools and authority to correct these misconceptions as they interact with patients. You may have just ruined some patient's enjoyment of their favorite, inaccurate television drama, but it is better that they realize the standards practiced on a TV show are fictional than that they believe your agency is not up to its job.

Aside from the practice of emergency medicine, most of what these stakeholders know specifically about your organization comes from the local media. From a short-term perspective, establishing and maintaining a professional relationship with editors and reporters in your service area will serve you well when the phones start ringing after an incident. If such professionals already have a relationship with you and know your facts can be trusted, you can count on them to seek you out first for information and to comment on an incident. This helps you control the public's image of the department by participating in what information gets reported by the media.

LONG-TERM GAINS

Even though EMS is very much a here-and-now type of profession, smart managers realize that successful operations today are the result of good planning yesterday. By the same measure, successful operations and public image in the future are to some extent shaped by what you do today.

Looking back at the annual health fair scenario, 50 years ago somebody had what has turned out to be a successful idea. Over the years, the event has become bigger, better attended, and eagerly anticipated by the community and your staff alike. With each passing year, details are collected, analyzed, and used to plan the following year's events. Information on what went well and what needs improving are shared with everyone inside and outside the agency who will be participating at this year's fair.

Promotional information given to the media emphasizes the historic nature of the fair, reminds readers of the previous year's successes, tells what improvements to look for this year, and thanks everyone who is responsible for making the fair happen. This cycle of planning, execution, review, and more planning will ensure many more years of success for the fair in this community.

Long-Term Gains Within Your Organization

When you share your public relations ideas and the reasons behind them with your department's personnel, be sure also to invite their feedback to help build community educational programs. Some older personnel have years of institutional and community knowledge. Younger personnel fresh out of the latest training academies are full of energy and new ideas. Enlist everybody to help you define the department's public image and the public information and education needs of your community. This participation results in a buy-in of the programs that result.

This buy-in also makes it more likely that your colleagues will willingly participate in the programs' execution. Their inside knowledge of the individual strategies and components of the program, the target audience, and the reasons for the outreach will make them better teachers in the streets, at community events, and in off-duty interactions with friends and family who are interested in their profession.

As personnel become more educated and participate in outreach programs, they become more aware of and dedicated to their agency's success. Now, they can serve as additional resources on the agency's behalf with partners and stakeholders. Through multiagency task forces, committee memberships, and community forums, they become additional voices promoting their department's goals as well as sensitive ears gleaning information important to the department.

Continually working toward and attaining public relations goals makes your superiors' jobs easier. A well-informed workforce gets along with each other and works more efficiently. A well-informed public lodges fewer complaints. A local press corps whose respect you have gained will carry that same respect to interactions with your superiors.

Long-Term Gains Outside Your Organization

Any successful EMS agency needs to be seen in a positive light by the community it serves. Public agencies rely on the goodwill of voters and elected officials for some or all of their ongoing funding. Private agencies funded by fees for services are dependent on customers calling them rather than a competitor. No matter where your funding comes from, you need to ensure that your agency projects an image of excellence in every way from patient care to management and spending.

Your job is to generate this information and get it out to the public. Nobody can know your story and reach your image-oriented goals better than you can. Not stepping up to this challenge means your public must look elsewhere for their information. They will look to the media, their friends, neighbors, family members, and doctors to assess your agency's competence. Even the most positive feedback from those other sources is unlikely to meet your desires and standards. Any negative feedback will increase your workload as you now have to allay those fears before you can proceed with telling your story.

A great saying in emergency services goes something like this: "A disaster is not the time to be handing out business cards." It is usually used in the context of planning joint training exercises, but it is equally valid for day-to-day operations. Keeping your strategic partners up to date on your agency and its operations and goals is just as important as keeping good relations with your personnel. Your personnel make your agency run at peak efficiency from the inside. Your strategic partners have the same effect from the outside.

Know your counterparts at outside organizations. This means more than writing down their names and phone numbers. Get to know these people so you can easily share information back and forth. Remember, although they are on the same scene with your agency, they likely have vastly different roles to play, some of which may conflict with what your people are trying to do. The more they know what you are trying to do, and vice versa, the better the scene will run, the better the public will be served, and the more likely it is that the camaraderie formed in the streets on daily operations will blossom into full-fledged cooperation when the big call hits.

Stakeholders are an extremely important audience, even though you don't have the same kind of daily interactions with them that you have with your personnel and partners. These groups and individuals have control over your financing, your legal basis to operate, and the scope of practice your providers are allowed to perform at various licensure levels.

You have several public information, education, and relations goals with stakeholders. First, they must remain informed about how the agency operates. This allows them to make informed decisions when considering funding and scope-of-practice issues.

Second, when they see the agency in your truthful, yet positive and efficient, light, it minimizes their temptation to dabble in operational matters. Individuals with oversight authority, particularly if they have been EMS providers, are eager to make operational suggestions. Having open lines of communication between the agency and stakeholders allows those concerned to see their suggestions in place or allows the agency to politely decline the suggestion without ruffling any feathers.

Third, your stakeholders are also your agency's ambassadors to the public, the press, outside government, and other more remote audiences. You want them to be well versed and able to speak knowledgeably about the agency over which they have some control. Likewise, they want to be informed so they can present "their" agency and leadership in the most positive light.

Although your stakeholders want to showcase the best in your agency, the press can be looking to do just the opposite. Scandal sells. Misuse of public funds is too juicy a story for any reporter to pass up. A citizen complaint to the media gets fully explored with the citizen before the reporter ever calls you. Despite reassurances of impartiality, after hearing only one side, which way do you think the reporter is already leaning on a story when he or she calls you?

Just as your EMS providers are trained to look for and treat the worst injuries and illnesses, reporters are trained to find a scandal that will sell papers or boost ratings. Unless you have established a trusting, working relationship with them beforehand, you will spend any interview in a defensive posture, looking guilty, and unable to advance the story in the manner you would like it to be seen.

Your goal is to have previously established the same kind of relationship with your local media that you want with your strategic partners. Approach the media with the idea of making them another partner rather than an adversary. That's not to say they will never question what you say. But, it will make the reporter more likely to call you with a desire to learn "what happened," rather than "what went wrong." This important distinction is made possible through good media relations.

CHAPTER REVIEW

Summary

Managing public information, education, and public relations for your EMS agency should be a big part of your job. With so many different audiences affecting your agency in so many different ways, keeping these groups informed and keeping your agency on message are crucial in one way or another to how you operate every day.

Just like arriving on the scene of a large incident if you are starting from square one, public information, education, and relations look like daunting tasks. But again, much like when managing a large incident, the work you put into preplanning will pay off in an operation that is self-sustaining and resolved successfully. Having a pre-incident plan to work from takes away much of the guesswork and wasted time.

WHAT WOULD YOU DO? Reflection

When Les took the EMS division chief job, he was prepared to lead operations, ensure good training, and provide his agency with the best equipment he could for the job at hand. He had not considered that public outreach would be such a significant part of his job. As someone who believes that pre-incident planning prevents poor performance, he looked for ways to become as knowledgeable about CHFD and public relations as he was about starting an IV.

To better understand how public relations works, he looked for books about marketing and the media. He had been writing patient reports and proposals throughout his whole career, but they certainly did not read like articles in the newspaper. He found news writing guides to make his press releases sound more like something a reporter would write.

Les consulted with everyone from his superiors to his staff to draft a list of all the stakeholder groups, strategic partners, public groups, and media outlets that impacted CHFD and that CHFD serves. By each name, he listed contact information, and noted each group's informational needs and how that group affected CHFD.

Les found a gold mine of information at CHFD headquarters. Past annual reports, budget documents, purchasing records, archived scrapbooks, photo albums, and veterans he interviewed helped him become an expert on CHFD from the inside. From the outside, Les researched local media archives and websites as well as the city library for news clippings and recordings about CHFD, from long ago to the present. Stories of change, growth, scandals, and triumphs all went into his files for future reference.

Review Questions

1. Identify potential stakeholders and partners.
2. What should a public service announcement accomplish?
3. What is the purpose of public education?
4. How are the various targeted audiences divided?
5. List public groups that could be target audiences for education programs.
6. What are some of the ways you can pique the interest and get buy-in from the press?
7. What are some of the areas to be proficient in as the person representing the organization?
8. What is the value of public relations?

References

Breakenridge, Deirdre. (2008). *PR 2.0 New Media, New Tools, New Audiences.* Upper Saddle River, NJ: FT Press.

National Fire Protection Association. (2005). *NFPA 1035: Standard for Professional Qualifications for Public Fire and Life Safety Educator.* Quincy, MA: NFPA.

Public Relations Society of America. (1982). "What is Public Relations? New York, NY: Author. See the organization website.

Yale, David R., and Andrew J. Carothers. (2001). *The Publicity Handbook.* New York: McGraw-Hill.

Key Terms

partners Persons or organizations outside the agency who help the agency do its job.

public education Making a general or specific audience informed of the existence of something, along with such details as how, when, where, and why it matters to them.

public information Making a general or specific audience aware of the existence of something.

public relations Helps an organization and its publics adapt mutually to each other.

public service announcements (PSAs) Message for the public good placed in print and electronic media at no cost.

stakeholders Persons or organizations that have a direct financial, legal, or operational impact on the agency, such as elected commissioners and governmental regulatory agencies.

targeted audiences A specific person or group identified by a common need or desire for the information being sent to them.

Principles of
Marketing

Objectives

After reading this chapter, the student should be able to:

2.1 Develop core concepts of marketing and how it relates to EMS agency operations.
2.2 Describe the different marketing environments that exist within an agency's jurisdiction.
2.3 Develop a SWOT analysis.
2.4 Discuss how to perform marketing research.
2.5 Explain how to target messages to markets.

Overview

This title identifies and offers examples of the informational and educational components that work together to form a comprehensive public relations plan. Capitalizing on successful strategies used in marketing and advertising, it explains the reasons why public information and education are necessary for gaining and holding the public trust.

Key Terms

brand	marketing	sample
macroenvironment	environments	SOAR
marketing	markets	SWOT
	microenvironment	target markets

WHAT WOULD YOU DO?

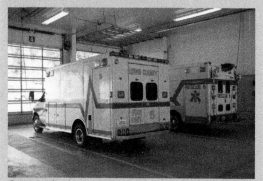

Communicating to your community is an important element for EMS agencies. *Courtesy of Ed Mund.*

To communicate effectively with his agency's various audiences, Les Phillips needs to learn more about the communities served by the Cooks Hill Fire Department, what kind of reputation and relationship the department has in the different communities, and how to best reach them with any messages he needs to distribute.

Questions

1. Can marketing principles be of any help?
2. What kind of research on the communities would be useful?
3. How can Les Phillips categorize and analyze that information to create an action plan?

■ INTRODUCTION

Marketing methods show you how to tell people your product or service exists, make them want it, make them need it, and then choose your product or service over another. You may wonder why EMS services need to be marketed. Most communities have a single 9-1-1 response agency with perhaps additional support agencies. EMS "consumers" do not get to choose who responds to their call for help. That is true, but how well have you addressed each of the four concepts—inform people, make them want, make them need, make them choose—with your stakeholders, partners and public? This chapter looks at using time-tested marketing principles and tools to tell your **target markets** that they want, need, and value your agency before and after the 9-1-1 call.

■ BASIC CONCEPTS

Marketing is the art of making people aware of the existence and value of a particular service or product. Marketing tools provide an excellent foundation that enhances the ability of EMS managers can reach any audience they choose with any message they wish to disseminate. You have an ongoing need to promote your services and their value to your public, your stakeholders, and your partners, all of whom you need to perceive your agency the way you wish. That requires proactive efforts on your part to **brand** your agency with the image you want it to have. See Figure 2.1.

MARKETING DEFINED

Markets are groups of actual or potential consumers of your service. Understanding who they

FIGURE 2.1 ■ Branding is used to identify and differentiate your agency.
Courtesy of Jeffrey T. Lindsey, Ph.D.

are and what they want is crucial to defining the message you send to each. The American Marketing Association in 2005 defined marketing in a way that describes what it accomplishes and who it benefits:

> Marketing is an organizational function and a set of processes for creating, communicating and delivering value to customers and for managing customer relationships in ways that benefit the organization and its stakeholders. (Sandhusen, 2008, p. 7)

The value delivered is specific to the organization. A breakfast cereal company may define value as delivering a high-quality, good-tasting, nutritious meal in a convenient package. A utility company may define value as the power always being available and ready for the consumer to use. An EMS agency may define value as a high-quality level of medical care delivered to the consumer 24 hours a day, 7 days a week.

HOW MARKETING RELATES

The process of "managing customer relationships in ways that benefit the organization and its stakeholders" (Sandhusen, 2008, p. 7) is where marketing most relates to EMS agencies.

Although many of the tools are the same, the process by which competitive commercial ventures and EMS agencies manage the relationship is different.

For example, when a cereal company creates a new cereal, it markets the cereal heavily to consumers, and then relies on customers to try the product, like it, and keep buying it. A marketing adage describes the process as creating an image that grabs the attention of a consumer on a grocery aisle, then using the consumer's desire for the product itself to make them look for it again.

The cereal company markets the new product by creating an initial interest, then continues to deliver product to meet ongoing demand. The initial marketing effort and expense can be short lived. Continued success is assured once consumers develop a preference and keep going back for more.

Note, how the roles in the relationship change. Initially, the company drives the product to consumers. Once the product has been established, the roles reverse. The consumer drives demand to the company to continue providing the product. Message management by the company changes from introducing a new product to differentiating a known product from its competitors.

For the EMS agency, the roles between provider and consumer do not reverse. The agency is always the driving force in managing the relationship because, unlike the cereal company, its business model is not designed around developing long-term relationships with repeat customers. The agency creates value, but without public outreach the only people who would know about it would be those comparatively few in the community associated with the agency or to whom the value had been delivered.

Marketing the EMS agency's value is important for all of its audiences. The public hopes for high-quality emergency medical care. The agency wants to manage that relationship in a way that reinforces that public perception. Benefits to the agency include a greater likelihood of people calling for appropriate help, overall public support for agency activities, and voter approval for funding requests if publicly funded.

The agency's partners need to know what value the EMS agency provides to the community. Outreach to partners makes it known where the EMS agency fits into joint operations and community planning. The agency benefits in turn by being perceived as a valued partner and called in to participate in community and event planning where the agency's expertise can be used and its interests watched over. Another benefit to the agency and its partners is more coordinated and better-managed multijurisdictional emergency incidents.

Some stakeholders have the authority to add and subtract funding from agency operations. Others have the authority to make changes ranging from minor to significant in how your agency responds to emergencies and how your personnel perform patient care. The core of the marketing message aimed at the stakeholders is the image of an efficiently run agency with well-prepared patient-care providers. Stakeholders will take pride in their ownership of an agency that provides high value for the dollars spent. Agencies that can properly manage their value message to their stakeholders will find those stakeholders less likely to intrude on agency operations.

Marketing the agency's value to its own personnel is also important. Managing the value message builds stronger relationships with agency personnel. Everyone wants to take pride in what they do and the agency where they serve. In the case of volunteers, that is something they can take home at the end of the day.

ESSENTIAL FUNCTIONS

Sandhusen (2008) describes the eight marketing functions that are essential to the success of any marketing efforts. Although written for commercial application, these functions also form a useful framework for managing the relationships between an EMS agency and its public.

Side Bar
Eight Essential Marketing Functions
• Buying
• Selling
• Transportation
• Storage
• Grading
• Financing
• Risk taking
• Developing marketing information

The first two functions—buying and selling—are grouped together as the Exchange Functions. In an EMS agency, the buying function involves determining what services are offered to the public. The selling function includes informing potential customers of what the agency can do for them when they call as well as which phone number to call depending on their needs.

Transportation and storage are grouped together as Physical Distribution Functions. Depending on the community, transportation of EMS resources includes ambulances, fire trucks, medic vans, SUVs, and other vehicles. (See Figure 2.2.) The EMS agency manager must be able to answer such questions from the public as "Why are two ambulances here?" and "Why did you bring a fire truck to an ambulance call?" The public also needs to know where to access emergency services if they cannot call 9-1-1. When the power is out and phone lines are down, where do they go for help? Where is their nearest EMS unit "stored?" Where do they access nonemergency services and programs offered by their local EMS agency?

FIGURE 2.2 ▦ Why an ambulance and a fire truck both respond to a medical emergency is a common question from residents. *Courtesy of Edward L Mund.*

Sandhusen (2008) groups the last four functions as the Facilitating Functions: grading, financing, risk taking, and developing marketing information. In the commercial world, grading means sorting products by quality and quantity. In an EMS agency, grading could be differentiating services by their level of service starting with nonemergency services and moving up the scale to treating true life threats. Nonemergency services could also be graded by whether they are medical services performed for a walk-in patient, or a 9-1-1 call, or perhaps the agency's participation in a public event.

Financing comprises the arrangements made to ensure the agency is funded for its work, and that it can pay all its bills. Depending on the type of agency, these funds could be tax monies, support from a nonprofit organization, corporate support, payments made by medical insurance, or any combination of these.

The agency takes risks when providing its services. How the agency is perceived by the public it serves can impact the odds of a lawsuit being filed after a particularly risky incident with a questionable outcome. Stakeholders who believe an agency is managing its risks properly are more likely to support rather than interfere in its operations.

Developing marketing information serves the seven other functions. It is the intelligence that EMS agency managers need to ensure they are providing value to their markets. Are certain sections of the community underserved? Is there a disconnect between the image the agency wants to project and what is being reported in the local media? Are incidents involving seniors falling, or kids not wearing helmets while riding bikes, increasing? Do people really know what a stroke is and when and why to call 9-1-1? Why did the last funding request fail at the ballot box? Good marketing intelligence gives EMS managers direction, helps them determine the content of a public relations campaign, and helps them monitor the progress of the campaign.

■ MARKETING ENVIRONMENTS

Marketing managers face a wide range of factors that influence how they create and carry out plans to reach their various audiences. These factors are known collectively as **marketing environments**. Each of these environments offers specific information about audience composition: their needs, attitudes, opinions, behaviors, and such. When crafting an outreach campaign, the EMS manager collects data from these environments to determine what message needs to be conveyed, what obstacles there may be to reaching the targeted audience, and what content or methods will enhance delivery of the message.

MICROENVIRONMENT AND MACROENVIRONMENT

Marketing environments can be divided into two primary sub-categories: **microenvironment** and **macroenvironment**. The microenvironment contains forces within and close to the organization that affect its ability to serve and do its job. These effects can be both positive or negative. For an EMS agency, this includes staffing, training, service delivery methods (apparatus, equipment, support infrastructure), and operational procedures.

When using staff to assist in a public outreach campaign, the campaign's goals must be successfully marketed to that staff so they become a positive force working for the goal. To get them to buy into your project, tell them what the reasons, content, process, and goals of the campaign are. Perhaps some additional training in public relations or public speaking will help the staff be more comfortable and effective communicating to the target audience.

The macroenvironment includes all the outside forces surrounding and impacting the agency. This can include regulatory, economic, financial, natural, demographic, technological, and cultural forces over which the agency has limited impact. The EMS manager must be aware of each force's impact on the agency and plan outreach efforts that speak to those impacts. These environmental factors are not static. They can change with economic conditions, population shifts, elections, and naturally occurring events. The EMS manager cannot control these environments, but with ongoing intelligence and outreach efforts he or she can be in a position to influence them to the agency's benefit.

ECONOMIC FORCES

The state of the local economy affects the funding of the agency, no matter the source. An EMS manager should know the recent history, current status, and forecast trends in the local economy in order to determine what marketing to stakeholders should be done. When money is tight, the message needs to promote an exceptional ratio of the value produced for the dollars received. In good economic times, the message may be softer, communicating "merely" an excellent return on investment. Thus, when the economy and money available are trending upward, the groundwork has been laid for modest and reasonable requests to improve service through increased staffing, capacity, services, equipment, and other fundable benefits. Whether funding is coming from a corporate board, nonprofit fund-raising efforts, or taxpayers, the principles remain the same. Manage the relationship with your funding stakeholders so they appreciate the value returned for their financial investment.

DEMOGRAPHIC FORCES

Demographic forces include population density, numbers, distribution, age, education, income level, marital status, religious affiliation, and home ownership. EMS managers use density, number, and age information to help plan geographic coverage.

Retirement community neighborhoods generate significantly more call volume than other neighborhoods with a mix of ages. Rural areas generate a fraction of the number of calls that the urban core does. The type and number of calls differ in elementary schools compared to college campuses.

This same demographic information is also useful in helping the manager create public information and education programs. The need is much more real to older populations than it is to teenagers or even young adults. Residents in retirement communities are generally supportive of EMS operations. Classes delivered to them on fall prevention, heart attack signs, and stroke recognition fall on receptive ears. When the classes are done well, the seniors are left informed, educated, and with an even higher opinion of the EMS agency.

Homeowners have a more vested interest in how their taxes are spent than do renters who never see a tax bill. Publicly funded agencies must establish and manage their relationships with the taxpayers who pay for them. The relationships need to reinforce the value received for the tax money contributed.

FINANCIAL FORCES

Economic forces affect entire communities; financial forces are more individualized. Although inextricably linked, they are not the same. When economic times are good, people have more money and may be more willing to support funding requests. Even when times are bad, jobs are scarce, and individual income is tight, sufficient funding must still be obtained to meet the service needs of the community. Even when their own finances have taken a hit, companies and taxpayers will still consider supporting a valued public service.

Some of the effects of the boom-and-bust cycle can be mitigated for publicly funded agencies with multiyear, voter-approved funding measures. When times are good and your messaging to the public has created a positive image, take advantage of this goodwill and turn it into an opportunity to generate income on a multiyear scale. Years later when the time comes to renew this ongoing funding, instead of asking voters for a new funding stream, you can simply ask them to continue what they have already been doing. Selling your need to voters for that will be easier than the first time around, even if economic and financial forces are working against you. If you make this request after investing several years on relationship building focused on value, it will be easier to accomplish. Knowing historic boom-and-bust cycles of the local industries and overall economic trends is key to the timing of your request and improving the odds of getting it passed.

COMPETITIVE FORCES

Competitive forces are usually looked at in the context of commercial enterprises. In metropolitan areas with multiple EMS services available, that context is certainly valid. An EMS agency in a multi-agency market must establish and maintain a competitive advantage in order to survive. This competition may be found less in the marketplace than in meeting rooms as your service negotiates for contracts with hospitals, 9-1-1 centers, local public entities, and other sources of patients.

Agencies that enjoy a monopoly on providing EMS services through contract or public-agency charter have other forms of competition affecting their operations. First, they compete with other agencies for skilled personnel. To counter that, EMS managers must first maintain a relationship with existing personnel that inspires them to speak well of their organization and even want to actively recruit on the agency's behalf. Public outreach focuses on the personal benefits of working for such a high-quality agency.

Best Practice

The State of Florida has a Strategic Plan that guides the State's EMS agencies and State's EMS office. As part of the plan, Goal 3: is dedicated to the promotion of EMS in Improving customer satisfaction through injury prevention, public education and knowledge of the EMS system. The subset of goal 3 is 3.3.

Objective

3.3: Identify, educate, and partner with all stakeholders (i.e. patients, health care providers, and hospitals) on Access to Care while continuing to share best practices to all EMS providers within the state.

Measure

% of EMS agencies that have representation on hospital committees

Reduction in ED overcrowding

Reduction in unnecessary ED visits
(Define unnecessary or non-critical conditions and reduce number of those visits)

Strategies

Identify top three issues affecting access to care and develop measurement tool to establish baseline for improvement.

Survey EMS agencies to determine how many have representation on hospital committees. Note: The Joint Commission (formerly known as the Joint Commission on Accreditation of Healthcare Organizations) does not require, but is a positive point in the accreditation process.

Publish the current Prehospital Best Practices paper and use it as a tool to educate all stakeholders.

Publish paper from the emergency nurses' perspective on ED overcrowding, including impact to ED due to Baker Acts (BA52) and psychiatric emergencies (lack of places to send BA52s).

Utilize mechanisms such as the quarterly EMS newsletter, Bureau of EMS (BEMS) website, and Florida EMS Community (FLEMSCOMM) to share best practices that are evidence and outcome based.

Identify funding mechanisms to support health fairs, statewide PSAs, and share best practices for health fairs.

Develop template letter for each EMS agency to send to their respective hospital administrators.

Educate the public about ambulance and ED use.

Publish/email quarterly/biannual report on hospitals and send to hospital administrators (Phase II of objective 6.3).

Lead

EMSAC Access to Care Committee

Resource

Florida Hospital Association (FHA)

PIER [Public Information Education and Relations]

Florida Association of EMS Medical Directors

Office of Trauma

Office of Injury Prevention

FENA [Florida Emergency Nurses Association]

Timeline

ongoing

Another competitive arena is funding, no matter what the source. Private or corporately owned agencies must compete with their company's other financial interests and obligations for their own budgets. Agencies funded by elected officials must compete for their share of designated tax dollars with other local jurisdictions such as schools, fire, police, roads, parks, and libraries. EMS managers must manage their relationship with these stakeholders to ensure that the information at their disposal during budgeting times enhances the agency's actual and perceived value in their eyes.

ANALYZE YOUR AGENCY'S SITUATION

The EMS manager gathers information about the surrounding environmental factors impacting the agency. These factors are analyzed with an eye toward providing direction for the manager's outreach efforts to the public, to partners, and to stakeholders. From a marketing point of view, no matter who the audience or what the interaction, the number one message to be communicated is that they are receiving good value for the dollars spent.

In the community, value gets defined one experience at a time as someone interacts with the agency. Thus, value may be defined as a fast response time; skilled, compassionate patient care providers; an important lesson learned in an agency-sponsored class or community event; and information the agency printed in the local paper. The EMS manager uses public relations to increase the number of value experiences occurring in the community, with partners, and for stakeholders.

Before the manager can describe and market the agency's value, he or she must use the intelligence gathered about the agency and its environmental forces to define what value the agency offers. **SOAR** and **SWOT** are two common management tools that provide a framework to guide this effort.

SOAR stands for Strengths, Opportunities, Aspirations, and Results. Like the SWOT method, the analysis begins by listing the organization's strengths and opportunities. Unlike the SWOT method, which then focuses great attention on overcoming threats and weaknesses, SOAR focuses energy on the positive aspects of exploiting strengths to create successes.

The SWOT tool analyzes the agency's Strengths, Weaknesses, Opportunities, and Threats. Simply put, a good SWOT analysis will provide the manager with a roadmap to follow that capitalizes on strengths, overcomes weaknesses, anticipates threats, and takes advantages of opportunities.

To do a SWOT analysis, take four sheets of paper and label each with one of the SWOT categories. As you go through the next four sections, list on each sheet every possible item you can think of for your agency, or the one with which you are most familiar.

STRENGTHS

The strengths and weaknesses section of the SWOT analysis looks inward at the agency itself. Its strengths are key parts of the value delivered. They may be skilled providers, state-of-the-art equipment and procedures, criteria-based dispatching, automatic mutual aid agreements, specialized services, medical direction, response times, accreditation, or cost-effective operations. These strengths build value and give the agency a competitive edge. They are the attributes featured and will assist in creating a positive image of the agency to all of its audiences.

WEAKNESSES

Weaknesses are any internal obstacles to success. Initially, the list may look like a mirror image of the strengths list. Strength = good patient care providers. Weakness = providers with poor skills. Strength = modern equipment. Weakness = obsolete or damaged equipment. Other weaknesses may be in areas such as communications, staffing levels, medical control, facilities, or multicall response capabilities.

Review the completed strengths and weaknesses lists. Think of ways to exploit the strengths to help define the agency's value. Work to overcome weaknesses that diminish the agency's value. The resulting picture of a strong, competitive agency that provides great value is what gets communicated in outreach to the agency's audiences.

Both the strengths and weaknesses lists change over time as a result of both internal and external influences. Hopefully, the former keeps getting longer and the latter shorter. Therefore, this analysis is not a one-time exercise. It is important to periodically revisit what the agency is doing right and what it can be doing better so the value message and the value reality continue to match.

OPPORTUNITIES

Where strengths and weaknesses are internal in origin, opportunities and threats come from outside the agency. The manager has limited control over either, but that's not to say there is no influence to be exerted on behalf of the agency.

What opportunities that are not yet being exploited are available to the agency? Is grant funding available? Can a local college do a better or cheaper job of initial EMS training for responders? Where are the most likely pools of potential employees or volunteers to be found? What existing groups in the community can help the agency in some nonresponse programs? What changing demographics can positively impact the agency's operations? Are there advisory or regulatory boards and commissions to whom the agency can send

representation? Have regulations or laws changed that can provide additional business or income? Can new technology help the agency do its job better? Would local media publish or broadcast regular guest contributions from the agency? The list can be as long as the number of opportunities to be found in any community. Examine the list for those opportunities that build on the agency's strengths and minimize the impact or provide a means of overcoming its weaknesses.

THREATS

Primary threats for a commercial entity include the state of the economy, competing products and services, and regulation. For-profit EMS agencies share these same threats right along with the cereal company, automakers, and banks. Not-for-profit and public agencies share the same economic and regulatory threats as their commercial colleagues. In addition, many of the specifics defined as opportunities can also become threats. Are population and demographic shifts reducing the need for the agency's services? On the other hand, are these changes overwhelming the agency's ability to cover all of its calls? Are regulatory changes costing the agency time and money for additional training and equipment? Are purchases driven by technology requirements seriously impacting the budget? Does someone at one of the local media outlets have a bias against the agency and a bully pulpit from which to express it? Each threat must be identified so a defense can be set up to minimize its effect on the agency.

As with strengths and weaknesses, these outside opportunities and threats change over time. The manager can influence these changes by taking advantage of opportunities and constructing defenses against threats. Others may come and go on their own. These lists must be periodically reviewed and updated as conditions change.

SWOT ACTION PLAN

Armed with the four lists, it is time to create a SWOT Action Plan to summarize your findings and lay the groundwork for future action. The Action Plan is a simple, four-box chart.

Side Bar

SWOT on Public Relations

Use this information to establish objectives, then develop strategies to accomplish them. Define objectives that can be achieved by:

* Overcoming *weaknesses* to pursue *opportunities*.
* Establishing a defensive plan to minimize *threats*.
* Minimizing vulnerability to *threats* by using *strengths*.
* Pursuing *opportunities* that fit in with the agency's *strengths*.

Example

Strengths	Weaknesses
• Experienced patient care providers	• Staff not trained in public communications skills

Opportunities	Threats
• Offer of weekly column in local newspaper	• Local radio commentator critical of agency's staff

Using these four elements of the SWOT analysis, the agency EMS chief establishes the objective of communicating the value of the agency's staff to the public in order to counteract the radio commentator's criticism. The chief's action plan includes these strategies:

* *Overcome the weakness* by teaching staff the rudimentary elements of written public communications. Columns written by

staff members are professionally edited before being released. The weakness has now been turned into a strength.
* *Establish a defensive plan* by assigning column topics that promote the agency's value being called into question by the radio commentator.
* *Minimize vulnerability to threats* by using topical, well-written columns.
* *Pursue opportunities* by accepting the paper's offer to print the guest columns.

Even though the radio commentator continues his criticism, the chief has used information in his SWOT analysis to create an action plan to offer another side of the story and communicate the agency's value to its public.

■ MARKETING RESEARCH

Identifying opportunities and threats from outside the agency requires conducting marketing research. Anecdotal evidence can suggest starting points, but often it is not thorough or accurate enough to use to develop action plans. The marketing industry has developed countless tools and techniques for collecting data. An overview of the processes can be useful for the EMS manager looking to better understand the surrounding target markets.

SEVEN STEPS

Acquiring and using intelligence through market research can be divided into a seven-step protocol. How much effort goes into each step can vary by the complexity of the research problem or by the scope of work that implementation requires.

1. Define the problem to be researched and objectives. The problem may be reactive: Why don't people call 9-1-1 immediately when having chest pain? Or, the problem may be proactive or preventive in nature:

How do we increase the number of children riding in appropriate car seats for their age and size? Once the problem has been defined, the resolution of that problem becomes the objective.

2. Conduct a SWOT analysis.
If an overall SWOT analysis has been completed recently for the agency, much of the internal information may already be at hand. Opportunities and threats specific to this objective may not be included, or may be discerned from other, more general items included. If no SWOT effort exists, then at least an abbreviated effort specific to the child seat objective needs to be conducted.

3. Design the research plan.
The weaknesses and threats section will point out what information is missing and provide a guide to where to find it. The opportunities section may reveal outside sources of the information, or at least others who can help obtain it.

4. Collect and analyze data.
The data generated will detail the level of awareness in the target markets researched. Analysis of the data can differentiate the awareness levels from generalized down to knowledge of age-appropriate specifics.

5. Create an action plan.
Use the data to develop an action plan that uses strengths and opportunities, minimizes threats, and improves weaknesses in order to reach the stated objective.

6. Develop a control system.
The true measure of the action plan's effectiveness is to create a control system with measurable benchmarks in between the current status and the fulfilled objective. These benchmarks will help identify which portions of the plan are working as designed, and which need to be changed.

7. Implement recommendations.
Use the action plan to launch the outreach campaign. As feedback comes in through public interactions, measure progress using the control system. As poor performance issues are identified by the control system, use more research, additional data analysis, or changes to the action plan to overcome them.

RESEARCH TECHNIQUES

Once a target audience has been identified, research will provide relevant information relative to that audience and the public outreach objectives. (See Figure 2.3.) Content gained and conclusions drawn are driven by the nature of the information sought. This nature can be divided into four main categories: objective, subjective, future oriented, and past experience.

Examples of objective information include demographics, finances, and economics. Subjective information includes data such as attitudes and behavior patterns. Future-oriented data would be useful when researching an audience's potential to change. Past experience data is more accurately measurable.

An important concept to understand when determining the scope of the research to be done is how to accurately obtain a **sample** of the audience. A sample is a limited portion of a larger entity. Public opinion polling or television's rating system are familiar examples of research via sampling. It would be impossible to individually collect and analyze information from 300 million people or millions of households. A representative sample is selected, then the results are extrapolated to be meaningful to the entire entity. Results can be biased depending on how the sample is selected, the data are collected, and the analysis is

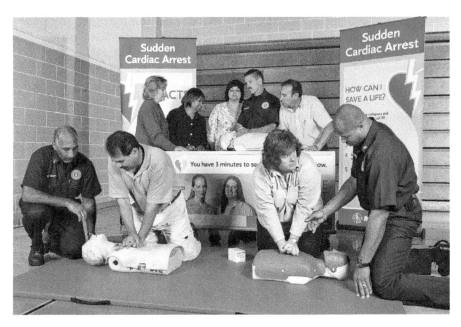

FIGURE 2.3 ■ Once a target audience has been identified, research will provide relevant information relative to that audience and the public outreach objectives. *Source:* Michal Heron/Pearson Education.

conducted. Samples can be either unrestricted or screened. Unrestricted samples are common with Internet-based surveys: There is no control over who gets the survey, or how many times any person can respond to the survey. Screened samples are carefully targeted to certain sample members chosen by specific demographic criteria and restricted to a single response.

The first of four common research methods is to collect data on areas of interest using literature searches. Today these are most commonly done via the Internet. A second research method is to analyze selected cases. This could include past behaviors, past experience on other issues, and even past attempts to reach this audience with a public outreach campaign.

Focus groups of representatives from the audience being researched is a third research method that can yield good data. The results can be biased by the selection process, who

gets selected to participate, the interaction with the moderator, and the skill of the moderator. On the other hand, focus groups offer a singular interactive component where issues and attitudes can be further explored.

The fourth common research method is some type of survey tool. Surveys can be conducted in person, by telephone, over the Internet, or by mail. Samples may be essentially unrestricted, as in a survey mailed to every residential address within a certain zip code, or phone calls to a single prefix. Screened samples can be defined by age, gender, household income, owner versus renter, private versus public employment, and a host of other demographic data that can be obtained from mailing list vendors.

Designing and conducting surveys can be complex. A few suggestions on survey design and content are offered below. More information may be obtained by taking a course on how to design and conduct effective research.

Survey design and content are key steps toward recovering accurate information in the research process. First and foremost, the survey content must be derived from the stated objectives of the outreach campaign. The purpose of doing the research is to gain information pertinent to accomplishing the outreach objectives.

Surveys can be highly structured or unstructured. Structured surveys have specific questions and predetermined answer choices. The information returned is uncomplicated and easily charted into most- to least-chosen answer. These are used mostly in written or Internet-based surveys. Unstructured surveys are generally conducted by an interviewer, either in person or on the telephone. A trained interviewer starts with a specific set of questions. Follow-up questions can delve deeper into the respondent's answers. Although this additional information may be of more value, it is also more difficult to categorize over the entire sample. Written and Internet-based surveys can also be a combination of structured and unstructured by allowing the respondent to add comments beyond simply selecting one of four available answers.

When preparing a survey, avoid unnecessary questions to keep the survey as short, relevant, and unobtrusive as possible. Don't ask a question or provide answers that a respondent may be reluctant or embarrassed to choose. Questions should be understandable and answerable by respondents from within their own experience.

Survey wording must be understandable to the target audience. This may be defined by the grade-level equivalent of the words used or the primary language spoken by the respondent. Jargon and words that can have multiple meanings should be avoided. Respondents should be able to understand the specific meaning of the entire question with no ambiguity. For instance, a question that asks "How many adults live in your home?" is less clear than "How many people aged eighteen and over live in your home?" Be sure the question points directly to the specific information desired.

At the same time, avoid writing questions that lead the respondent to any other answer than that which would come from their own unencumbered thought process.

Questions can be open, with no suggested guidance or answers for the respondents. Multiple-choice questions offer the respondent several choices. This makes the results easier to tabulate. It also can make the survey less relevant if the respondent would not be inclined to select one of the answers offered.

The order in which questions are asked can improve responder interest and help ensure completion of the survey. Do not ask questions that might make the respondent uncomfortable up front. Place them well into the body of the survey, to be answered after the respondent has already accepted the task of answering the survey. Consider the influence of a question and its answers on the next question. Arrange questions by topic in a logical order.

Survey Questionnaire

This survey should take less than 5 minutes to complete. The survey is part of a research project for Chief Jeffrey Lindsey of Estero Fire Rescue, Estero, Florida 33928.

1. When an emergency vehicle approaches you from the rear with its lights and sirens on, according to Florida state law you should:

____ Pull to the right curb	____ Pull to the left curb
____ Stay in your lane	____ Pull to the closest curb
____ Stop in your lane	____ Drive faster to keep in front of the truck
____ Don't know	____ Cross the yellow line into oncoming traffic

2. You are at an intersection and your light is red. A fire engine is coming from behind you. You should:

   ____ Go through the red light to allow the fire engine to go through
   ____ Stay in place
   ____ Pull into the intersection to let the fire engine go through
   ____ Don't know

3. You are approaching an intersection. Your light is green. A fire engine is approaching from your right with its lights and siren on. The engine has the red light. You should:

   ____ Proceed forward since you have the green light
   ____ Stop and wait for the fire engine to go through the intersection
   ____ Don't know

4. How many years have you lived in Florida?
   _____

5. Where do you reside (city/town)? _____
   _____

6. Are you a year-round resident? ____ Yes
   ____ No

   If not, where else do you reside? _____
   _____

DATA ANALYSIS

Information gained through research becomes useful through coding, tabulation, and analysis. Coding involves creating categories to plug in data received. For instance, age, income level, and children under a certain age in the home could be categories. Tabulation involves separating responses into the categories and then expressing totals as numbers or percentages. Analysis evaluates the tabulated and coded findings as they pertain to research objectives of the original outreach campaign. Going back to the child seat example, coding data for children of car seat age and tabulating their numbers and locations tells the researcher how many parents with children are in the target audience and their location.

■ TARGETING

Target audiences are high-potential groups of people with common characteristics and needs that distinguish them from other groups. Running-shoe companies target different types of athletes for their various shoe products. Automakers use market research to define target audiences for their brands and models. An EMS agency with bicycle helmet or child care seat programs targets them to parents and grandparents of school-age children. (See Figure 2.4.)

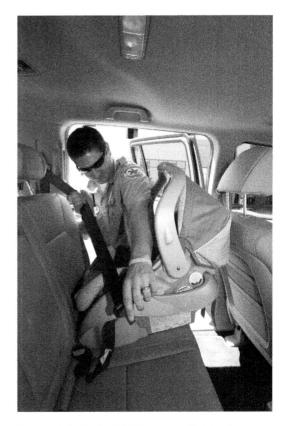

FIGURE 2.4 ■ An EMS agency with bicycle helmet or child car seat programs targets them to parents and grandparents of school-age children. *Source: © Bryan E. Bledsoe.*

Market research identifies where your target audience can be found and offers some clues on how to reach them. In addition, the marketing industry has generalized information on how to reach target audiences.

HOW DECISIONS GET MADE

Whether consciously or not, people go through a process before making decisions. The complexity of the process and the time it takes to reach a decision are affected by many factors. A husband and wife may debate for an hour over whether or not to call 9-1-1 after the onset of his chest pain. On the other hand, she will call immediately the moment he collapses onto the floor.

Decisions start with the recognition of a problem. *I'm hungry. I'm thirsty. My chest hurts and it's hard to breathe. Wow, that's a lot of blood! Our neighbors had a car wreck and their children were seriously injured with no car seats.* Problem recognition leads to an information search. What's in the refrigerator? Is there any beer left in the cooler? Is this really a heart attack? I wonder if this will need stitches? Let's take a look at what kind of car seats we should have for our kids.

Next, alternatives are explored. *Should I really eat any more today? There's no more beer—what else is left? Maybe it's heartburn from the pizza I had at lunch. Is a bandage good enough? The kids are almost big enough, so do we really need to spend that kind of money for such a short time left?*

Finally, the decisions get made. The EMS manager's objective in the public relations campaign is to get the target audience to make the recommended decision at the appropriate time. In effect, this will short-circuit the second and third stages and get people to make the right decision without wasting time or getting distracted by less frequently recommended alternatives.

People's behaviors are influenced by interpersonal and intrapersonal variables. Interpersonal variables are the influences of large groups, such as the person's culture, age, social class, family group, and gender. Intrapersonal variables make an individual more or less likely to be receptive to suggestions. These variables include motivation, perception, attitudes, and lifestyles. As the EMS manager crafts the message to a target audience, it is important that the message contain information that speaks to the variables that have been identified through the market research.

TARGETING MESSAGES

Just as surveys can be broad based, tightly focused, or somewhere in between, outreach messaging can be as widely or sharply targeted. Mass messaging would employ an undifferentiated strategy in which the message and target are broad. A newsletter with agency news, a calendar of all upcoming public events, and free blood pressure check locations would be mass-mailed to every address in the zip code(s) served by the agency. With a differentiated strategy, a single-topic message would be sent out by mass distribution. A public hearing announcement on an upcoming ballot issue would be mailed to every address in the agency's area. Some would reach affected voters, many would not. In addition, to improve the number of people reached, the same announcement could be posted on the agency's website, sent as a bulk-addressed email, posted on the agency's social media site pages, and distributed by other electronic means.

A concentrated strategy sharpens the focus even more. This is also known as niche marketing. A specific message is directed to target audiences that share an interest in the information. The announcement of an upcoming bicycle-helmet-fitting event could be distributed to the local elementary schools, day care centers, and mailing lists of parent–teacher organizations.

An even more narrowly focused strategy is called micromarketing. A specific message is targeted to a specific group. Notification within a retirement community of blood pressure checks in the clubhouse next Tuesday is an example of micromarketing.

INFORM, PERSUADE, OR REMIND?

When developing objectives for a public outreach campaign, an early decision to be made is whether the intent of the message is to inform, persuade, or remind the target audience. Informing means making the audience aware of the existence of whatever the message is about. For example, the agency offers free blood pressure checks at its EMS stations, or a crew will go to elderly people's homes free of charge and assess for tripping hazards.

Persuading is generally used when the audience is being asked to make a decision, consider an action, or change how things have previously been done. The audience must also be informed because it is through presentation of information that the case is made for taking action. For example, "Time is your enemy, so call 9-1-1 now, not an hour after the pain starts," or "Falls can alter your lifestyle and shorten your lifespan, but are preventable through this program."

Reminding can involve repeating something the audience already knows but forgets easily or chooses to ignore. The importance of getting your blood pressure checked and managed is one example. The potential to maintain mobility and add years of enjoyment to your life through a fall-prevention program is another. The fire service has maintained a successful reminder program for years with its campaign to tie changing smoke detector batteries to the biannual clock changes. (See Figure 2.5.)

FIGURE 2.5 ▪ The fire service has maintained a successful reminder program for years with its campaign to tie changing smoke detector batteries to the biannual clock changes. *Source: Gary Ombler/Dorling Kindersley.*

The style of the message has a bearing not only on how it is written. It also can influence how much and what type of research needs to be done. External data for an information campaign can be nothing more than a geographically or demographically based mailing list. Persuasion may require psychographic research. Looking at run data to see what kind of preventable issues are generating repetitious calls for the agency or problems in the populace would be an example of using reminder research to help target the right message to the right audience.

MARKETING CONTROL SYSTEM

Continuing a process that does not lead to accomplishing objectives is a waste of time, effort, and resources. However, where the process derailed may not be obvious without application of some checks and balances. This is where a control system comes into play.

Control systems can only be created when there is a clear understanding of the expected results and the steps identified in the action plan to reach them. Controls offer benchmarks to ensure that everything which was supposed to happen does happen, at the right time and in the correct order. When errors arise, the control system will identify what went wrong. Data from the original research and possibly new research can be analyzed to suggest a new approach. The action plan is then altered to take advantage of this new information. The control system will also be altered to correspond to the action plan in its new form.

For example, an EMS agency launched a public information campaign to increase the number of residents of a retirement community who attend the free monthly wellness checks in the community clubhouse. Informational flyers were produced and placed in the clubhouse. For the next 2 months, the numbers attending did not increase. One of the control system elements was to monitor the number of flyers picked up. A count showed that of the 50 flyers placed, 48 remained after 2 months. A query to the clubhouse manager revealed that residents only come to the clubhouse if there is a specific event, and the community has had the best response when they mail notices. The agency changed its action plan to mail the flyers and include a coupon for a free gift. The control system was modified to monitor the number of new flyers with coupons that were redeemed.

CHAPTER REVIEW

Summary

EMS agency managers can use many principles and elements from the marketing industry as they reach out to their customers. Essential functions of the marketing business can help the managers learn about the marketing environment in which they are operating, including the macro- and microenvironments economic conditions, demographics of the area as a whole and specific pockets within, financial health of customers, and the competition they face for funding, business, and staff.

Conducting a SWOT analysis on the agency will be an eye-opening experience the first time it's done. It should also cause three immediate reactions in the manager: a desire to take advantage of unrealized opportunities, an impatience to turn weaknesses into strengths, and an unwavering quest to eliminate threats.

Marketing research tools and techniques will lend valuable assistance to the manager in identifying and dealing with the outside opportunities and threats. They will also help the manager focus on getting the message right. Targeting tools will help the manager direct messages to the right audience.

Managers who use marketing principles to guide outreach efforts will be more successful in communicating the value of their agency to all of their audiences.

WHAT WOULD YOU DO? Reflection

Les did some Internet searching and browsed bookstores for information on marketing. He really had no background in this profession and hoped the concepts and processes would translate easily into his world. He soon realized that the income tax preparation firm and his EMS agency trying to reach its various audiences were really trying to do the same thing. Both were offering a set of associated services. The generalized and multiple targeted markets or audiences for that service could be identified. Marketing research would reveal how to reach the audiences, and how to craft the messages to take advantage of some environmental factors and allay fears from others. Marketing principles were an effective framework do meet his needs.

Les performed a SWOT analysis for the agency. He was determined to be as inclusive as possible, so he included others in the agency at all ranks to help him draft the strengths and weaknesses section. He also enlisted some trusted partners and stakeholders to get their perceptions of the agency's strengths, weaknesses, opportunities, and threats.

With the SWOT analysis completed, Les drew up a public relations action plan containing public information and education outreach programs. He categorized them based on acute versus ongoing need, timeliness to other seasonal or community events, complexity to accomplish, and budget needed to initiate. He then prioritized the programs based on need, time to dedicate, and realistic expectations of accomplishment.

Review Questions

1. Define what marketing is in the context of this chapter.
2. What are the two marketing environments? Give at least three examples of each.
3. What is the difference between SOAR and SWOT?
4. What is the seven-step protocol for acquiring and using intelligence through market research?
5. What are target audiences?
6. There are three choices to make in regard to the target audience when developing objectives for a public outreach campaign. What are they?

Reference

Sandhusen, Richard L. (2008) *Marketing,* 4th ed. Hauppauge, NY: Barron's Educational Series, Inc.

Key Terms

brand Name, images, and perceptions developed to identify and differentiate a company, agency, or product.

macroenvironment Forces external to the organization that influence its ability to perform.

marketing Organizational function and processes for creating, communicating, and delivering value to customers and for managing relationships in ways that benefit the organization.

marketing environments Forces that influence the manager's ability to attain communications objectives.

markets People or organizations with an interest in or need for a product or service, or past and present consumers of a product or service.

microenvironment Forces within the organization that influence the organization's ability to perform.

sample A limited portion of a larger entity.

SOAR Strengths, Opportunities, Aspirations, and Results

SWOT Strengths, Weaknesses, Opportunities, and Threats

Public Information and Education Tool

3 CHAPTER

Objectives

After reading this chapter, the student should be able to:

3.1 Explain the four steps of creating a Public Information and Education (PIE) Tool.

3.2 Adapt a model PIE Tool to a specific department.

Overview

This title identifies and offers examples of the informational and educational components that work together to form a comprehensive public relations plan. Capitalizing on successful strategies used in marketing and advertising, it explains the reasons why public information and education are necessary for gaining and holding the public trust.

Key Terms

criteria-based medical
  dispatching
message

public safety access
  point (PSAP)

two-tiered response
  system

WHAT WOULD YOU DO?

It is important to have the right tools to do the job.
Courtesy of Jeffrey T. Lindsey, Ph.D.

Throughout his career, Les Phillips has relied on good training and appropriate tools to do his job. This has always created a comfortable space for him to do his work. This combination has been his path to acquiring new skills. The marketing research he has already done has been valuable training and helped him create an action plan. Now he is looking for the tools to help him create and implement specific public information and public education programs.

Questions

1. How can he create such a tool?
2. How can he make it flexible enough to cover all contingencies?

■ INTRODUCTION

Sometimes simple tools help us do our jobs. How would we listen to lung sounds without a stethoscope? Or check pupils without a penlight? Or write a report without a pen or pencil? Sophisticated tools makes it easier to do our jobs better. An automated blood pressure (BP) monitor is easier to use than the manual process with a stethoscope and BP cuff. Patient care report forms that let us fill in the blanks rather than record every detail from memory let us record the incident faster, more accurately, and in greater detail. A public information and education tool for your jurisdiction offers the same speed, accuracy, and effectiveness benefits when you have a **message** to communicate as does a good, fill-in-the-blanks form.

■ FOUR-STEP PROCESS

The goal of a good public information and education tool is to get specific messages to a specific demographic in a manner and language that an audience will understand. Whether the desired result is to inform or educate, the process is the same.

The public information and education tool is an infinitely alterable template based on taking the four actions described below. The message can be varied to fulfill different needs. For example, the audience will likely differ according to your messaging goals. The content must effectively speak to the message's intended audience(s). Finally, how the message is delivered is impacted by time, the message itself, the most effective means of reaching the intended audience, and often the budget.

DETERMINE YOUR MESSAGE

Start with a goal that states what information needs to be communicated. Look at the types of communications, miscommunications, and questions that arise in the media, in the department, in public, and during interactions between responders, patients, and family members every day. Any time you hear a question raised, consider it a potential need for additional outreach to describe the role and impact of your agency and its providers. Identifying issues and putting them into broad categories, such as the following, will help you develop your plan as you work through the rest of the tool.

Definitions/Perceptions

Expectations about local EMS agency performance are greatly influenced by the media and the entertainment industry. These expectations can be made more realistic through information and education outreach programs. Examples can include the following:

- Seasoned responders see that the public does not differentiate between levels of training and assistance that can be offered. In their eyes, everyone is a paramedic. This causes confusion over wait times for care, why a fire truck or police car responded to their aid call, and why their chest pain was not resolved in 60 minutes, minus 12 minutes for commercials.
- Stakeholders with budget authority see money being spent and review statistics about how that funding was used. What they do not personally experience every day is the one-on-one value the local population receives with each and every call the agency runs. Information and education can bring their awareness to a level where they truly understand the personal connection between budget dollars and patient interactions.

- Law enforcement officers often work the same scenes with fire, EMS, and rescue crews. Although public service is the tie that binds them all, each has a different job. There are times when one's job can interfere with another's ability to do theirs. A common example is at motor vehicle collisions. EMS crews are taught to position their vehicles on the scene in such a way as to create a safe working environment, even if it means closing the roadway altogether. Law enforcement wants to keep traffic flowing to minimize secondary collisions in the backup. EMS crews focused on scene safety and patient care may drive through or park on top of evidence that law enforcement wants to preserve. All parties sharing information and education about needs and priorities will reduce friction and improve multi-agency operations.

System Descriptions

What happens in your jurisdiction when someone calls 9-1-1 for a medical emergency? What most people know is that they make the call and within a few minutes help arrives at their door. Do they know all the preceding steps that take time, planning, money, and training to accomplish what looks to be so simple? Without that knowledge, the public and your stakeholders cannot fully appreciate everything being done on their behalf. This diminishes the perceived value in their eyes.

- Trace the call from the patient's phone through the enhanced 9-1-1 system, if appropriate, to the **public safety access point (PSAP)**. Describe what 9-1-1 does for them, how it is funded, and how it works.
- Educate the public on how the PSAP works internally so they understand that the time the call taker spends on the phone with them enhances the service they will receive, not delay it. If you are using a **criteria-based medical dispatching** system, explain how

using it to best match the caller's needs and the resources being dispatched benefits both your agency and the public.

* According to a report released by the Federal Communications Commission in February 2007, less than 95 percent of the households in the United States had some kind of basic telephone service, either landline or wireless. In Arkansas, the state with the lowest percentage in the nation, the number was less than 88 percent. Educate the public on how someone with no telephone access can summon help in an emergency. This information is also good to know during natural disasters when broad-based phone service is diminished.

System Component Identification

* Once the call is dispatched, who responds, with what kind of training, and in what type of vehicle? Describe who is standing by ready to respond, how many resources are protecting your jurisdiction, and how many emergency calls they respond to each year. The people paying your bills want to know that their money is being spent not just on response capacity, but also on actual usage.

* If you are operating a **two-tiered response system**, explain how it maximizes resource utilization. Be sure to allay fears that the care being sent is substandard compared to their expectations.

* If your agency operates concurrently with another public or private responder on initial response or transport, your public will want to know why multiple units are at their house. Your stakeholders will want to be sure they are not paying for duplicate services. Providing good information to both audiences will show how the arrangement is working on their behalf both economically and medically.

Financing Methods

Whether your funding comes from taxpayers or a board of directors, these audiences want to be sure their money is being used wisely. At the same time, they may not even realize all the different sources you tap into to lessen their financial burden. Although this can bring up questions about why you cannot get more outside funding, it also gives you the opportunity to demonstrate your good stewardship of their dollars.

* Show your funding sources the creative ways you make their money go farther through bulk buying agreements, off-peak and peak load scheduling to reduce labor and overhead costs, and nurse-on-call diversion programs that give callers with nonurgent needs the option of talking with an emergency department nurse rather than dispatching EMS units.

* If you are a public agency seeking additional funding from taxpayers via a bond issue or an increase for taxes you can collect, be specific about how the money is spent. If your agency has a past performance of always keeping its financial promises on previous ballot issues, be sure to feature that history in current outreach efforts.

* Document the work that goes into applying for grant funding, the type and number of grants received compared to the number applied for, and how grants have reduced your need for other one-time or ongoing funding.

Noteworthy Accomplishments

Here is where you can really show each of your audiences how much value they are receiving from your agency. Communicating these milestones is where you show stakeholders, partners, the public, and your own personnel that they are receiving exceptional value from your agency. Everyone associated with your agency likes to see good news reported about it. Everyone helping to fund your agency will appreciate knowing they are paying for a quality operation staffed by outstanding professionals.

Regulatory stakeholders will be reassured that the agency is providing quality care.

* Recognize, in person and in the local media, professional achievements by agency personnel.
* A word about the use of grant funding to upgrade the agency's operations or capabilities at no cost to the stakeholders is always welcome news.
* Systems status goals achieved, such as meeting response-time benchmarks, exceeding patient care targets, and reliable in-service availability of units shows a well-managed agency full of dedicated people.
* Selection for research projects speaks highly of your responders' professionalism and the agency's reputation. Follow-up with a report on the research results is a reminder about the agency's value.

IDENTIFY YOUR AUDIENCES

When considering what message needs to be delivered, you must also give equal consideration to the message's intended audience. These audiences were defined within four broad groups: stakeholders, partners, the public, and employees. A message may be targeted specifically to one audience or, with modifications, to multiple audiences. When the message is in response to a question that has been raised, the target audience becomes obvious: whoever asked the question. However, don't stop at the obvious answer. If that person or the group represented by the person does not understand what you do, then maybe other important audiences are equally uninformed.

Most of your informational and educational outreach messaging will be aimed at the general public, or certain subsets of public groups. These audiences have the greatest need for your agency's services and, yet, the lowest level of comprehension about how it happens. They also have the greatest need

for education on how to avoid the need for EMS services through trauma prevention and healthy lifestyle programs.

A public education program about trauma prevention through children wearing bicycle helmets can serve as an example of how a single topic can be messaged in different ways to different audiences. Your messaging goal is to show that bicycle helmets make a positive impact. The public message will educate parents about how helmets can save your child's life and how to get one at little or no cost through the EMS agency's program.

The message to partners will be to inform other public agencies, such as law enforcement, fire services, and public works that this program is underway. Give them supplies of a brochure about the helmet distribution program to give to kids they see riding bicycles with no helmets.

Employees also receive a supply of brochures to hand out as they come across kids with no helmets. They can also offer them to parents during interactions on EMS calls—especially ones involving trauma to children.

Stakeholders are first informed of the effort along with the reasons and costs behind doing it. After-action messaging educates stakeholders on the successes of the program according to benchmarks established, such as helmets distributed, reduction in injury severity, and reduction in trauma calls related to bicycle crashes.

The stakeholders' message is then repackaged for dissemination to the public featuring the initial goals and results achieved. The stakeholders' message was centered around the success of the program from a cost–benefit point of view. Using the same information, the public message defines the success of the program in more human terms, such as public participation, reductions in the number and severity of injuries, and potential lives saved. By the end of the program, the public education goal of raising awareness that bicycle helmets make a positive impact on the community has been achieved, and every audience important to the EMS agency knows it.

CRAFT THE MESSAGE

In order to achieve your communication goals, message content must be relevant to the audience and crafted in terminology the targeted audience understands. Just as you would not discuss medical terminology and drug doses with grade-school children, it would be equally inappropriate to use puppets and cartoons to present your budget request to your board of directors or elected commissioners.

The two key considerations when crafting the message are these:

- The language used
- The applicability of the content to communicating your message to the target audience

Language

In this context, language can refer either to the dialect being used—English versus Spanish versus Mandarin—or to the scholastic level of the words and sentence structure. Community research will be instrumental in defining which dialect(s) need to be used to communicate your messages to certain public audiences. Producing your message in multiple languages produces two immediate benefits. First, it will increase the possibility of reaching more people. Second, it can improve the credibility of your agency and message because you respected the target audience enough to use its language.

From a scholastic point of view, it is important to remember that if the words you use are "over the heads" of your intended audience, your message will be lost to them. On the other hand, if the readers sense you are talking down to them, your message will not be received correctly either.

Newspapers, periodicals, and websites are good sources for determining what level of language usage is appropriate for each of your target audiences. Messages to the general public should use words, sentence structure, and paragraph lengths that match your local newspaper's feature news reporting. Messages to partners and your own employees should be written at a level common to the industry journals and training materials they already read. Look to stakeholders' communications with your agency to learn the correct content level for communicating with them.

CONSIDER CONTENT

Once the language questions are answered, it is time to consider content. All content must drive the reader toward your communications goal for that message. Supporting material is important. Distractions are a waste of time and can divert attention from your message.

- Data are generally an important component of most messages. If A (department participation) + B (helmet giveaways) = C (more helmet use), and C = D (fewer injuries), then A + B must also equal D. Using data in a public message about the bicycle helmet program could look like this: *Cooks Hill Fire Department has seen a 17 percent decrease in injury calls for children on bicycles since the bicycle helmet giveaway program started.*
- Financial impacts are often important elements of message content. Commonly seen phrases include *"This funding cut will result in . . ."* or *"This grant money will allow us to . . ."* or *"Thanks to the levy support by our voters, we will be able to continue. . . ."*
- Historical "then versus now" comparisons can be used to make a point in your argument for or against something: *"Our budget request is higher than last year's because even though our call volume has decreased by 3 percent in the past year, overall costs have still gone up due to a doubling in the price per gallon we pay for fuel in the ambulances and a modest step increase in paramedics' wages."*

- Historical comparisons also mark progress in patient care areas important to the public, stakeholders, and employees. *"Prior to this new technology and protocols, 24 percent of the patients we saw with this condition died. Today that number is down below 10 percent and still falling."*
- Trends can be used like a historical comparison to demonstrate repeated patterns of behavior, types of calls being run, measurable increases or decreases in call volume, or to call attention to an uptick in patients presenting with a certain common set of signs and symptoms. A message to partners in public health could advise of a trend showing influenza-type patients calling from a concentrated area or single apartment complex in much higher numbers than elsewhere in the general population. Law enforcement partners need to know about geographical areas showing dramatic changes in assault or drug overdose patients.
- Projections are the heart of financial negotiations, whether the audience is the general public whose support is needed to fund the agency, the stakeholders who control the agency's budget, or employees with whom you are negotiating compensation and scope of work. Because these are projections and not facts, they are open to interpretation according to the writer's and readers' own point of view. Projections must be based on verifiable data, historical comparisons, and trends to stand the test of audience reaction and be credible.
- Actions considered and actions taken should also be tied to data, and where possible historical comparisons and trends. *"Peak call volume time has lengthened by 30 minutes in the past month to an average of 9.5 hours out of every 24. The agency considered the need for additional resources on the street and has concluded that the current trend is consistent with annual call histories for this time of year and projects the call numbers to drop back again in 60 days as in years past. Therefore no additional resources will be needed at this time."*
- Testimonials are the bread and butter of commercial marketing campaigns. A drug company

marketing to seniors will find an actor who looks and sounds like the healthiest possible example of their target market. The actor will swear to the rejuvenating or lifesaving or life-restoring effects of the company's product. What consumers wouldn't want to then run to their physician and add years to their lives, too? The thing is testimonials do work, when planned and executed properly. Testimonials can help EMS agencies successfully convey important messages to the public. *"I'm so glad I called 9-1-1 in time!"*

- The main interaction between an EMS agency and its various audiences is that agency's employees. Much of this interaction takes place during an emergency, where there is no time to get past first impressions. Use public information about the human side of the agency so the public and your partners' first impression of your agency through your people takes place before they meet on the scene. Human interest stories in the media about fantastic saves that feature the personnel rather than the medicine add a human element that introduces your crews before they even hit the streets. Feed local media press releases about milestones, certifications, licensures, new hires, promotions, and anything else about the human side of the agency.

DELIVER THE MESSAGE

Message delivery is dependent on several factors, including the goal of the message itself, the intended audience, budgets, and logistical challenges. For the public and partners, the mass media is the quickest and least costly means of spreading a message over the widest possible geographic area and number of audiences. The relationship the agency shares with local reporters and editors will have a significant impact on the agency's ability to use the media where and when it wants.

Targeted written communications are effective with specifically targeted audiences. For a large group, such as a neighborhood association or a local school's parent–teacher association, personalized letters can guarantee the highest level of reach and, hopefully, readership.

Direct mail is an alternative to mass media for ballot issue information and generalized public health messages aimed at populations according to geography. The goal may be to alter behavior, inspire behavior, solicit funding, or garner support. Whatever the goal, the message must be written to target the audience being reached with that goal clearly stated.

Messages delivered via the media or mail are also good candidates for placement on your agency's website. The website offers another means of widespread message dissemination. It also allows you to focus on the goals of your message in your other outreach materials. Keep your messages simple and to the point, but with enough information to allow readers to make the decision you seek. At the same time, include references to the website for detailed information for anyone wanting to know more, either before or after they've made a decision.

Best Practice

There are a number of training opportunities for public information officers (PIOs). The PIO Social Media Boot Camp is one such training group. One of the great aspect of this site is that it offers the training for free. There are a number of resources

you can use including webinars, policies, and other resources to enhance your capability as a PIO.

Source: piosocialmediatraining.com

When dealing with stakeholders, employees, and certain messages to specific partners, targeted written or oral presentations can be the most effective. Be sure to have written handouts to leave behind in support of the information presented orally. Take notes on questions asked, and whether answered fully or not, and send each audience member a written follow-up with this additional information.

Side Bar

Using the PIE Tool Sample

Sample Use of Public Information and Education (PIE) Tool in a Prehospital Setting

Step 1: Message Goal

A countywide EMS system needs to communicate the positive results of a 6-month trial

"Nurse-on-Call Diversion Program." During this period, callers identified by the public safety access point's (PSAP's) criteria-based dispatching system as having nonurgent medical needs were offered an opportunity to have their calls transferred to the local hospital ED nurse rather than send an EMS response to the caller's location. Callers had the option to refuse, accept, or, once accepted, change their minds and request an EMS response after talking with the nurse.

Message Content

* During the study period, 363 callers to the PSAP who would have previously had an EMS team dispatched to their location for a nonurgent medical need were instead forwarded to the hospital's ED to consult with a nurse. In 340 of the 363 calls, the nurse consult satisfied the patient's needs and resulted in no response by EMS. For the 23 callers who remained concerned, an

EMS crew was dispatched. All 363 events resulted in positive outcomes for the callers.

Step 2: Identify the Audience(s)

- General public
- Other PSAPs in the state
- Other EMS systems in the state
- Local governance for the system
- Individual providers within the system
- State Department of Health

Step 3a: Craft Message to the General Public (Information)

- Describe how EMS system operates.
- Detail anticipated results—why the study was started.
- Detail then-versus-now results on:
  - Patient outcomes
  - Cost of the diversion versus cost of dispatching units
  - System status improvement with fewer low-priority calls

Step 3b: Craft Message to PSAPs, Other EMS Systems, Local Governance, Providers, State Department of Health (Education)

- Detail anticipated results—why the study was started.

- Describe how the study was funded.
- Detail then-versus-now results on:
  - Patient outcomes
  - Cost of the diversion versus cost of dispatching units
  - System status improvement with fewer low-priority calls
  - Potential to remain at current service and cost levels longer due to reduction in low-priority calls.
- Share lessons learned to assist others in replicating the study, or implementing diversion into their system.

Step 4: Deliver the Message

- Inform the public:
  - Mass media
  - Oral presentations to business and service groups
- Educate PSAPs, EMS systems, local governance, and providers:
  - Via trade journals
  - Oral presentations at conferences
  - Some influence via mass media
- Inform the Department of Health:
  - Oral presentation to appropriate administrators and committees
  - Regional planning documents submitted to the state

CHAPTER REVIEW

Summary

The real purpose and value of the PIE Tool are to take the guesswork and intimidation out of starting a public information or education program. Start by outlining the tool's contents. Identify all the potential audiences you may face or want to reach. When a communication need arises, pull out the tool. Set your message's goal, select the correct audience(s), craft the message to communicate your goal in a manner

the audience(s) will understand, and deliver the message via a means they can embrace.

The contents of the four steps of the PIE Tool are not cast in stone. The contents are designed to be as comprehensive as possible, but certainly can have items added or subtracted to any degree at any time. The PIE Tool is a living document designed to help you do your job easier, faster, and more effectively.

WHAT WOULD YOU DO? Reflection

Les made a list from memory of all the questions he had to look up answers to from the past week at work. These included interactions in his office, phone calls, discussions in meetings, and queries from reporters. From these questions he drew up a list of all the audiences who had been represented by the questioners: newspaper, employees, superiors, state regulators, a local senior center, and a private ambulance service partner. As the audience list took shape, it inspired him to add more, like the local police department, television station, school administration, and others. He made a note to himself to look for reference materials on writing in different styles, for different media, and to various audiences. Next, he made a list of local media outlets, local printers, and direct mail outlets and made an appointment to meet with city and county elections officials to learn more about direct mail for ballot issues. Finally, he sent an email to the CHFD webmaster to learn more about using the agency's website.

Review Questions

1. What are the four steps in the PIE process?
2. What are the two key considerations when crafting the message?
3. Name at least three factors upon which the message delivery is dependent.
4. What are the two immediate benefits of producing your message in multiple languages?
5. What are the four broad groups of audiences?
6. Give at least two examples of noteworthy news item to communicate for your agency.

References

Mund, Ed. (2008, August). _Out of Reach: 9-1-1 Misses 6 Million Households._ Daytona Beach, FL: Public Safety Communications, APCO International.

Key Terms

criteria-based medical dispatching Sending resources to the scene of a medical emergency call based on the perceived needs as determined by comparing the caller's information to a set of standard criteria.

message Information to be communicated to an audience.

public safety access point (PSAP) Central location where calls for emergency help are received and emergency responders are dispatched.

two-tiered response system Emergency medical response system where calls are triaged by criteria-based medical dispatching into Basic Life Support (BLS) or Advanced Life Support (ALS) categories. BLS-designated calls are responded to by emergency medical technicians at Basic and Intermediate levels. ALS-designated calls are responded to by emergency medical technicians and paramedics.

CHAPTER 4 # Audience Identification

Objectives

After reading this chapter, the student should be able to:

4.1 Define the four main groups of audiences.
4.2 Identify different audiences within each of the four main groups of audience.
4.3 Explain the differences between reporters, editors, and columnists.

Overview

This title identifies and offers examples of the informational and educational components that work together to form a comprehensive public relations plan. Capitalizing on successful strategies used in marketing and advertising, it explains the reasons why public information and education are necessary for gaining and holding the public trust.

Key Terms

personnel

targeted public groups

WHAT WOULD YOU DO?

Tracking data is an important element of a public relations campaign. *Courtesy of Jeffrey T. Lindsey, Ph.D.*

As Les Phillips goes through his daily phone messages and emails, he starts to notice some patterns emerging. Some people call more than others do. He seems to be a primary recipient on emails from several individuals with whom he routinely works closely, and on the cc: list from other people he does not know but who work for agencies and companies related to his in different ways. It seems to Les that there is valuable information to be gained, but he is not quite sure how to capture or use it.

Questions

1. Can Les create a "Need to Know" catalog of entities and individuals he needs to communicate with routinely?
2. How does he categorize these entries in a way that will help him remember what information each needs or wants from him?

▨ INTRODUCTION

Being able to identify the people you want and need to reach is a fundamental element of any public relations effort. Some groups self-identify by asking for information. A local reporter calls with questions. A local health club owner inquires about the process for installing automatic defibrillators in her facility and getting her staff trained to use them. An investigator from a state regulatory agency queries purchases made.

Others need to be sought out, cataloged, and periodically touched by relevant messages. You want voters to understand how their tax dollars are being spent. Collaboration with local law enforcement officers on response procedures to potentially dangerous scenes ensures well-coordinated action. Elected officials need to know the benefits, consequences, or both of proposed legislation that may affect your operations and public safety.

Creating a robust catalog of previously identified audiences offers at least three immediate advantages:

1. The process of making and updating the list keeps all audiences high in your awareness level.
2. Your risk of being blindsided by someone or a group you were unaware of is dramatically reduced.
3. When you have a message to send to a group, individual, or population, contact information is already at your fingertips.

Audiences are categorized into four broad groups: stakeholders, partners, **targeted public groups**, and **personnel**. The press can also be considered an audience group when you are offering background or historical information.

However, your primary interest in the press is not as an audience, but as a conduit for disseminating your message.

■ STAKEHOLDERS

Stakeholders have the power to control how your agency operates through legislation, funding, rules, and regulations. Stakeholders can be groups or individuals. They have the authority over how the agency functions as a whole, how much money it has to spend, what areas it can serve, how the agency and individual members are licensed, and who leads the agency.

WHO ARE YOUR STAKEHOLDERS?

Publicly funded agency stakeholders start at the grassroots level with voters who pay tax money to support the agency and run up the political food chain to elected officials who direct how that money is spent. Privately funded nonprofit agencies can have the same relationship with their contributors and board of directors. Corporately owned agencies have stockholders and a board of directors to answer to financially.

Whether public or private, anyone providing emergency medical services is regulated by various levels of government. This is true whether the services are provided to the public at large or within the confines of a corporate workplace.

EXAMPLES OF STAKEHOLDERS

Federal/National Level

The Centers for Medicare and Medicaid Services (CMS) is a federal agency within the U.S. Department of Health and Human Services. CMS is the national clearinghouse responsible for regulations and payments related to the care of patients covered under Medicare or Medicaid health care plans.

CMS operates as a stakeholder in two respects: funding and regulation. Ambulance fees are regulated and paid through CMS's fee schedule for transporting covered patients. Agencies that accept funding from CMS are then bound to adhere to a host of operational regulations, most notably the Health Insurance Portability and Accountability Act (HIPAA).

The U.S. General Services Administration publishes what are informally known as the "KKK" standards. Formally called the "Federal Specification for the Star-of-Life Ambulance, KKK-A-1822F," the standard is reviewed and revised every 5 years. The standard's purpose is to establish minimum standards for new ambulances built on an original equipment manufacturer's chassis in order for the vehicle to be authorized to display the "Star of Life" symbol. In actual practice, the standard is used as the baseline for manufacturing ambulances and medic units in the United States.

By virtue of its role spelled out in the U.S. Constitution, Congress is where federal laws are enacted. Government agencies will then adopt regulations that impact how EMS agencies operate, but these rules must have a basis in law as passed by Congress. HIPAA regulations from the CMS serve as an example of a federal agency promulgating regulations in order to implement new law. The Ryan White Law is an example of where the law itself has a direct impact on EMS operations, telling agencies and personnel how to balance their need for information with the patients' privacy rights in circumstances involving bloodborne pathogens.

The U.S. Department of Homeland Security (DHS) is both a stakeholder and a partner for EMS agencies. In its stakeholder role, DHS creates incident management procedural standards and requires their use by any agency that accepts federal funding. Through its subsidiary U.S. Fire Administration (USFA), DHS offers grant programs designed to help first responder agencies acquire and maintain equipment and training.

The National Highway Traffic Safety Administration (NHTSA) is an operating administration of the U.S. Department of Transportation that has been generally considered the lead federal agency for emergency medicine since the 1970s. Through its various programs, NHTSA offers guidance and standards for EMS training, education, certification levels, workforce levels, system design, and preparedness. In addition to its own work, NHTSA acts as a conduit for the EMS industry to other associated federal agencies and workgroups.

Although primarily a resource for fire services, the National Fire Protection Association (NFPA) serves as an EMS stakeholder group. On one hand, a significant percentage of the EMS delivery in the United States is provided through a community's local fire department. These fire service personnel have been trained according to NFPA standards in a fire department that operates under the guidance of NFPA standards, and respond in vehicles designed and built to NFPA standards. Although these standards do not have the force of law, they are generally regarded consensually as the professional standards for the fire service. In the context of case-law precedence in the civil legal arena, NFPA standards carry nearly the same weight as laws.

Another area where NFPA standards affect EMS agencies is *NFPA 1917: Standard for Automotive Ambulances*. These standards were developed in cooperation with NHTSA, fire services, and other interested parties.

State Level
Just as Congress passes laws on a national level, the state legislature is responsible for passing laws in each state. This legislative body—which goes by different names in different states—is responsible for health care, licensing, training, funding, and other laws

affecting how EMS agencies operate in that state.

Each state has one or more departments that, in similar fashion to federal agencies, turn laws into rules and operational procedures. Each state's Department of Health, or Public Safety, or Licensing, or some other name sets rules for education, training, scope of practice, equipment, and workplace standards as well as licensing of agencies, vehicles, and personnel. In addition, state rules and regulators carry some type of enforcement role to ensure that EMS agencies and personnel comply with all laws.

Some states have a separate agency that acts as a conduit for federal funding and is dedicated to social services that provide state funding directly. Federal Medicaid funding that is administered by each state is an example of a federal dollars conduit program. With all funding comes rules on how it is to be spent, what individuals and services are covered, and how the EMS agency bills and is reimbursed for taking care of individuals' needs. States have discretion on how federal funds are distributed and who is eligible. Programs can vary widely across states. (This topic is covered in detail in *EMS Finance* by Dennis Mitterer.)

Some pension systems may be operated by the state, especially those that provide coverage to volunteer responders. The pension board sets rules for eligibility, financial, duration, and work-related requirements for participation, and determines where incoming funds are invested to keep the system solvent.

Some type of state-provided medical insurance for on-the-job injuries may cover paid EMS responders just as it would any other workers. Premiums paid into a state fund by workers and their employers cover costs for treatment and rehabilitation, and can provide disability pensions when private coverage is not already available. Volunteer responders may also have the same type of coverage in some states, although it may be through a separate system or state agency.

Local Level

With every level of government comes the opportunity to pass more laws, make more regulations, and write more rules. That can affect how your service operates, depending on whether you are located within the jurisdiction of an unincorporated or incorporated area, county council, county board of commissioners, or city council. If your agency provides services across municipal and county lines, your agency is then subject to some statutory control by various government agencies. Business license requirements, local tax levies, local taxing authority grants, and road restrictions are just a few of the ways a governmental entity can influence an EMS agency.

Providing EMS care in the field requires allowing responders some level of autonomy to perform certain skills and interventions on patients. Patient care guidelines often start at the state level with scope of practice models for various certification or licensing levels. These models are put into practice and personnel training is accomplished at the local and regional level through EMS councils, boards, and training programs. These stakeholders are responsible for ensuring that training is completed, responder skills are good, and patient care is performed correctly. Regional or county EMS councils may also be responsible for drafting patient care procedures, county operating procedures, and protocols that guide patient care in the field.

The medical program director (MPD) is responsible for approving what patient care procedures, protocols, equipment, and training are required for EMS crews to work in the field under his or her medical license. In this respect, the MPD is a stakeholder with the power to add or subtract approved procedures, drugs, or devices. The MPD might also have disciplinary power over individuals practicing within his or her jurisdiction.

Through approval of protocols or standing orders, the MPD defines whether EMS responders work under an on-line or off-line medical control system. In an on-line system, field personnel are required to call medical control for permission to treat a patient with certain drugs, equipment, or procedures. Off-line medical control allows responders to perform certain tasks, such as start IV lines, administer drugs, or use medical monitoring equipment, without first asking permission under the authority granted in protocols or standing orders.

Every EMS agency falls under the jurisdiction of some type of governing body. It may be comprised of elected officials, corporate officers, local citizens, or some other group. The governing body has authority to hire and fire the agency director and perhaps other senior staff. This group sets budgets, approves capital purchases, sets goals, and defines future plans for the agency to achieve.

Best Practice

The following is an example of how a stakeholder meeting produces goal-oriented results.

FICEMS National EMS Stakeholder Meeting—March 17–18, 2010

The Federal Interagency Committee on Emergency Medical Services (FICEMS) held a National EMS and 9-1-1 Stakeholders meeting on March 17–18, 2010 in Washington, DC. The meeting was sponsored by the Department of Homeland Security, Office of Health Affairs. DHS understands the critical role EMS plays in health care, public health, and public safety by frequently providing immediate life sustaining care and making decisions with limited time and information. Because EMS is a critical point of access to the health care delivery system for all Americans, FICEMS has taken the initiative to promote evidence-based health care delivery and regional systems of care.

The FICEMS was established by the Safe, Accountable, Flexible, and Efficient Transportation Equity Act: A Legacy for Users (42 U.S.C. § 300d-4). FICEMS is charged with coordinating Federal EMS efforts for the purposes of identifying state and local EMS needs, recommending new or expanded programs for improving EMS at all levels, and streamlining the process through which Federal agencies support EMS.

At the FICEMS Stakeholders meeting, FICEMS leadership presented a brief overview of current Federal EMS and 9-1-1 related activities, responded to questions and listened to the opinions and ideas of national organizations and interested individuals about national EMS priorities and future directions. FICEMS proposed the meeting as one way to improve communications between EMS stakeholders and Federal agencies.

The meeting was intended to solicit suggestions about national EMS priorities and future directions, but not to establish a group consensus. Whereas the detailed meeting minutes will be available later, the following is a very brief overview of some recurring comments. This is not an exhaustive list of the suggestions:

1. *EMS Standardization*—Some stakeholders suggested there should be enhanced national standardization of the nomenclature and training of all prehospital EMS providers as well as critical care levels, emergency medical dispatch and medical direction. There were recommendations to review areas in which there has already been nation-wide standardization of state-licenses such as drivers licenses and nursing licenses.

2. *Facilitate the Collection, Access, and Use of Research and Evaluation that Informs Clinical Practice*—Suggestions included the posting on www.ems.gov of a consolidated list of recognized peer-reviewed EMS journals that publish EMS research. Some suggested there should be incentives for EMS systems to adopt NEMSIS compliant data collection and reporting. There were suggestions that an EMS-specific national Institutional Review Board would facilitate additional research and would help to ensure patient discharge information is available to researchers.

3. *Safety*—Ensuring the safety of EMS providers and their patients was an issue frequently mentioned by stakeholders.

4. *Funding*—Many stakeholders stressed the importance of dedicated funding to support clinical care initiatives and for prehospital EMS including supporting the cost of readiness . . . not just transport. Some suggested a series of meetings throughout the nation focused on funding and sustainability of EMS systems.

5. *Lead Federal Agency*—Many stakeholders suggested the need for a Federal lead agency with authority to establish a strong agenda and to serve as a liaison with Congress. Some of its suggested activities include data and research, providing funding, creating partnerships, ensuring the health and safety of EMS providers and patients, supporting EMS education, improving the EMS workforce, and establishing standards.

6. *National Performance Standards*—Some stakeholders encouraged the development of mandatory national standards and encouraged the Federal partners to pursue rigorous, evidence-based standards and guidelines for EMS and 9-1-1 services and the use of incentives to help ensure compliance.

7. *Vision for Next Generation EMS*—Stakeholders suggested the need for a national consensus on the future vision of EMS . . . one that would enable all to speak with one voice, while still recognizing State, regional, and local variations.

8. *National Responder Database*—Some stakeholders felt there is a need for a federally operated National Responder Database, based on uniform responder definitions to enhance surge capacity, verify credentials, and track line of duty deaths and injuries.

9. *National EMS Academy*—A National EMS Academy was suggested by some to mirror, for EMS, the mission and purpose of the National Fire Academy including Federal oversight.

The more detailed minutes of the Stakeholder Meeting will be made available later. The input of the Stakeholders meeting will be reviewed by the Technical Working Group with recommendations to FICEMS. The stakeholder, input will also be made available to the National EMS Advisory Council and to others.

Source: www.ems.gov/pdf/FICEMS_Stakeholder_Mtg_ExecSummary.pdf

For publicly funded agencies, taxpayers are an important stakeholder group. They want to know their tax dollars are being spent wisely just as much as they expect an immediate and effective response whenever any one of them calls for help.

Depending on where your agency is located, the local city or county public health department may be a stakeholder, a partner, or have no impact at all. In some areas, EMS services fall under the jurisdiction of a public health agency, which makes the agency a stakeholder controlling how the EMS agency does its business. In other areas, EMS services and public health are separated, but they often work together as partners to conduct wellness campaigns, help at-risk populations, and reduce workloads. In addition, there are areas where the EMS agency and local public health have no real knowledge of each other, what services each provides, or how they operate.

For public and private EMS agencies with paid responders, an employee union may be a significant stakeholder to consider. The union has influence over scope of work and how agency funds are spent on payroll and benefits during contract negotiations. That influence continues during the life of the contract. EMS managers considering changes that would affect scope of work, pay, overtime rules, or any other aspect covered in the union contract will have to consult the contract and the union before implementation.

■ PARTNERS

Simply put, partners help your agency do its job, day in and day out. (See Figure 4.1.) These individuals and organizations often will be labeled as stakeholders because they, like you, have a stake in how your agency does its job. However, because they are also in the trenches with you, side by side, putting themselves on the line, it really is more accurate and respectful to call them partners.

WHO ARE YOUR PARTNERS?

One key partner is the Public Safety Access Point (PSAP), or as it has more traditionally been called, the dispatch center. Without the PSAP to answer 9-1-1 calls for help, to dispatch units, to be a resource for units in the field, and to coordinate other agencies on the same incident, EMS responders' jobs would be considerably more difficult and dangerous.

The stakeholder's role of DHS has been discussed, but the department is also an important partner for EMS agencies. Through its subsidiaries, such as the Federal Emergency Management Agency (FEMA) and FEMA's National Emergency Management Institute, training, education, and model procedures are available to first responders nationwide.

The NHTSA, as mentioned, is also a stakeholder. However, it is an important partner for

FIGURE 4.1   Partners help your agency do its job, day in and day out. *Source: Richard Logan/Pearson Education.*

EMS agencies in several areas, too, including the following:

* Federal-level research on standards, practices, educational, and workforce issues affecting EMS agencies nationwide
* 9-1-1 PSAP initiatives
* National data collection and dissemination

EMS agencies could not do their jobs without support from their public safety partners. Law enforcement helps restrain combative patients, secure scenes, provide traffic control, and deliver a host of other assistance, including an extra pair of hands for a short-staffed EMS unit working up a critical patient.

One of the first true EMS operations in the United States began in a city fire department. Today approximately half the EMS providers in the United States are still fire based. For those who are not, their local fire department responders are trusted colleagues offering more than just a firefighting response. They also have rescue capabilities, can respond to hazardous material and other special circumstances, and provide tremendous assistance at motor vehicle crashes.

Transporting EMS agencies play a role in many communities. Some are first-response units that also transport patients. Others respond with nontransporting fire-based EMS agencies to provide patient transport to the hospital. In some jurisdictions, a public EMS agency and private transport company mutually respond to 9-1-1 calls to increase the level of service available, and the latter frees up public response units for the next call by transporting the patient.

Air medical resources offer speed and range where ground-based transportation is either unavailable or will take too long to transport a critically ill or injured patient. Both fixed wing and rotary wing aircraft operate inter-facility transport services and emergency transport from the scene.

Hospitals are important partners for EMS agencies, especially when it comes to ground or air transport. Hospital capabilities directly impact transport destination choices and transport methods depending on the patient's condition. In many communities, a local hospital serves as the base of operations for the local and surrounding EMS agencies, providing medical control on a patient-by-patient basis.

Like EMS, home health and hospice agencies perform in-home patient care. Because of their activities, EMS agencies' run volumes can be reduced as home health workers manage patients' medical needs. When an EMS response is needed for an acute condition or for patient transport to further care, EMS crews arrive to find the patient already under professional care, and they typically receive better patient information than normally found when responding to a private home.

In addition to providing guidelines in their stakeholder role, regional/local EMS councils collaborate with EMS agencies to help provide initial and ongoing training, equipment research, and advocacy to state-level stakeholders on behalf of member agencies.

Every EMS agency manager knows that the MPD has great authority over the agency's responders. The smart manager also sees the MPD as a strategic partner who is dedicated to helping the agency do its best work every day. Working together, the MPD and agency management can exert quality control, solve equipment problems, examine standard of care issues, expand off-line medical control, and enhance scope of practice to provide better services faster in true medical emergencies.

Partnering with public health agencies and professionals gives EMS agencies more tools to use in serving their communities. In partnership, in-home wellness programs reduce call volume and expenses, intervention programs get repetitive patients off the streets and into needed care, and massive public vaccinations can be accomplished more quickly and thoroughly.

Unions are both stakeholders and partners for wise EMS managers. When an issue comes up, or a change is being considered, union reps have the inside knowledge and can take the pulse of the workforce quietly before the issue becomes public and posturing replaces cooperation. Let the union do its job, and it will help you do yours.

Schools collaborate with EMS agencies to offer public safety education at all levels. From grade school first aid classes to high-school-level vocational training, local schools offer EMS agencies an opportunity to spread their messages throughout the community and to recruit tomorrow's workers while still at an impressionable age. After high school, professional EMS training for those looking to get into the profession can be obtained at local colleges, or through the agency itself.

Local vendors, especially in smaller, more close-knit communities, are predisposed to want to help their local public safety agencies. In volunteer agencies, it is likely that many of the responders leave their jobs or businesses to grab a rig and run calls throughout the workday. These types of local business friends can be cultivated to provide materials, labor, and equipment on short notice and after hours. Having an open account at a locally owned hardware store and the owner's phone number can really make a difference at 11:00 p.m. when you need shoring material or extra digging tools in order to save someone.

Hospitals can be much more than just a destination for your patients. Seek their help to train responders on patient care. Work with them to prepare mass casualty plans so all your units in the field and everyone back at the hospital are on the same page when disaster strikes. Use their expertise in patient care, disinfection, and equipment to help your agency get better in all areas.

Clinics and self-standing emergency rooms offer alternatives for patient care when your primary hospital is on divert, or a mass casualty incident has overwhelmed your hospital's resources. Create agreements in advance, with clinic callback procedures and protocols from your MPD that allow transport of some types of patients to these types of facilities.

Local or nearby military resources can be made available under certain circumstances. The U.S. Coast Guard has watercraft and aircraft that can assist with water rescues and patient transport when no other private resource is available. Working through your local EMS council or some other governing body, the prudent EMS manager will explore what military resources are available, under what circumstances they can be utilized, how to contact them in an emergency, and how to have agreements in place up front to ensure a response when it is needed.

Advocacy groups work to further their members' agenda with the public and, most often, with governing bodies. Ally yourself with reputable groups whose interests mirror or at least closely match your own. Your agency may not have much of a voice in the halls of power at the city council, county council, or state capital, but your voice combined with other public safety and health groups with similar interests and goals will rise above the din and be heard.

Whereas equipment and techniques get all the glory, at the heart of any EMS agency is the people who make the agency operate, treat patients, and save lives. Those people need extra help on occasion, and at some time everyone will have to be replaced. Partnering with scouting to develop an Explorer or cadet program helps youth get a firsthand look at a possible career, and can provide the agency with additional staffing to help its public performance. Not everyone has to be EMS certified to be useful. Explorers or cadets can provide staffing at health fairs, traffic control at accidents and public events, and assistance with reporting and recordkeeping, to name just a few tasks.

Volunteers are also the backbone of the EMS system in the United States. Whether serving as certified EMS responders, or helping out in myriad administrative and non-EMS roles, volunteers from your community help the agency achieve its mission every day.

Although apparatus vendors may not seem to be obvious choices for this category, they are important partners helping you serve your community. Cultivate a relationship that is more than just commercial transactions. Offer to help evaluate new products. Let manufacturers demo your new medic unit before placing it in service. When the time comes when you need a part *now,* being on good terms with your suppliers can reap rewards.

Communities host a wide range of charitable organizations, civic groups, and clubs. Although the end purpose for most is to do good work in the community, local business and community leaders who look to each other first when in need also populate them. Membership in selected groups helps raise the visibility of your agency with these people and helps ensure their support and assistance when needed. You may be looking for a location to host a public event, or support for an upcoming funding levy, or assistance in spreading the word about a new program. The people who are already trusted in the community and who share a common bond become additional credible mouthpieces for your message.

TARGETED PUBLIC GROUPS

Members of the public can be looked at in their entirety, and as different special-interest groups. (See Figure 4.2.) The overall public for an EMS agency is anyone in its service area, whether they live there, work there, come into the area for some other reason, or are just passing through.

After this, the public can be divided into as many separate groups as there are collections

FIGURE 4.2 ■ Members of the public can be looked at in their entirety, and as different special-interest groups. *Courtesy of Jeffrey T. Lindsey, Ph.D.*

of people. Service clubs care about their specific charities and community projects. Advocacy groups are passionate about a cause. Neighborhood associations are people who care about their little corner of the world and are concerned about how well and quickly their local EMS responders can serve them. Your job is to identify all the groups in your service area, learn who the leaders are, know what their goals and ambitions are, and find a way to align their interests with yours. This will increase your agency's positive image in the community and help you disseminate your public health and safety messages.

WHO ARE YOUR PUBLIC GROUPS?

Targeted risk groups exist to reduce preventable tragedy. As such, many have goals and support causes on which it is easy for an EMS agency to find common ground. Often the targeted risk has something to do with preventable death or injury to the public or particular population groups. Working together to reduce preventable death and injuries is a natural fit for any EMS agency.

Perhaps the most well-known pediatric risk groups are those advocating for and providing bicycle helmets and proper car seating for children. Public safety agencies often partner with a local charitable organization to provide free or reduced-cost helmets and car seats, along with the training for parents to properly select and fit them to their children. Other groups seek to prevent child abuse or help children and parents deal with catastrophic pediatric diseases.

Targeted risk groups for adults run the gamut from gun safety to impaired driving, healthy lifestyle promotion, and risky behavior reduction. Preventing harm from occurring reduces the demand on EMS systems and community public health services. Each illness or injury prevented equals one person not calling for service.

As adults age, a whole new set of problems arise as driving skills deteriorate, the ability to live independently is reduced, circulatory problems increase, and the simple acts of standing and walking without falling become ever more challenging. Identify and collaborate with targeted risk groups working with these populations. Your agency's skilled care providers can help with outreach and education, and preventable medical and trauma crises can be reduced, your agency's reputation improved, and call volume lowered.

Advocacy groups operate in a fashion similar to targeted risk groups in that they have pet projects or causes. The main difference is that advocacy groups put more emphasis on promotion than prevention. Examples of advocacy groups include those dedicated to raising funds and finding cures for different diseases or mental health issues. Other groups seek to stop self-destructive behaviors, such as Mothers Against Drunk Drivers—a clearinghouse for information on ways to stop impaired driving. A local business group such as Rotary is an advocacy group that could raise funds to help a targeted risk group advance its efforts. Advocacy groups can also contribute physical labor to a specific project, but the bulk of their public outreach is financial support for targeted risk groups who are actually doing the work on behalf of their constituencies.

As the EMS manager identifies targeted risk and advocacy groups in the community, he or she must also evaluate which groups would benefit from the agency's participation. This can take the form of taking a membership in the group and becoming an active club participant.

It can also just be a matter of offering expert information and guidance, or maintaining a presence at community events sponsored by various groups.

Side Bar

The State of Alaska developed a document called The Injury Prevention Program Inventory http://hss.alaska.gov/dph/emergency/ems/Assets/Downloads/InjuryPreventionProgramInventory.pdf. This document is a collection of single-page informative sheets. Each sheet contains information about a program and how that program operates; its costs, methods of delivery, and success; as well as other information. To assist you in finding the information about programs you can conduct in your own communities, the index page helps you locate information about a category, such as drinking; a target population, such as children's programs; goals; and so on. The inventory is an excellent tool to assist you in the development of your programs for targeted audiences.

PERSONNEL

As the EMS manager puts great focus on meeting his external messaging challenges, it is important to not overlook the need to also share this information internally. (See Figure 4.3.) Open communication within an agency complements your external messaging efforts. Public information and education constitute a job for everyone wearing your agency's uniform because anyone the public sees in uniform is the voice of the agency. The EMS manager needs to be sure that all personnel at all levels are delivering the same message so they are all working to promote the best interests of the agency as defined by the manager.

Because EMS agencies operate in a top-down management style, the EMS manager

FIGURE 4.3 ■ As the EMS manager puts great focus on meeting external messaging challenges, it is important not to overlook the need to also share this information internally. *Courtesy of Jeffrey T. Lindsey, Ph.D.*

and senior administrators must first agree with what messages the agency will send to its audiences. Then management needs to stay on message, speaking with one voice to subordinates, while providing the in-depth background of how the message came to be when the inevitable questions or disputes arise from subordinates.

The EMS manager should educate managers and supervisors so they have the same in-depth knowledge of the decision-making process that led to a particular outreach message. Their subordinates, too, will present questions and challenges. The EMS manager must ensure that answers are based on the same facts and that the message goes forward as intended.

Field staff is really the front line of both offense and defense for the agency's message. On offense, staff needs to know what the message is, and when or where they are expected to be an agency mouthpiece. For example, an agency has launched a new blood pressure screening service at all its stations. Information pamphlets about the service are distributed to field providers who are told to hand them out to every senior citizen they see during their shift.

On defense, having all field staff conversant in the agency's public messages is critical for when citizens approach them. It does not matter if the citizen approaches a veteran or a brand-new hire; the citizen believes the responder is the voice of the agency at that point. Having everyone conversant in the same message ensures a consistent image in the public's eye.

While empowering staff to speak on behalf of the agency, be sure to offer guidelines on when and where such action is appropriate. The agency should have clearly delineated when to respond to a question versus when to refer it to an agency manager or public information officer. All personnel must understand what type of information they can give out, when it is allowed, and to whom.

FRIENDLY PRESS

The press is an audience all by itself. EMS managers need to understand the difference between reporters, editors, and columnists.

Reporters consider their participation in world events from the third-person perspective. That means they write news as an observer telling the story, rather than as a participant in the story. They seek to be objective, presenting only the facts, and try to show all sides of the issue being examined. EMS managers need to understand this methodology. They can never try to force the reporter to write only one side of the story, or ever penalize the reporter for including the opposition's position. To do either will be to risk souring an important relationship. It may also increase the likelihood that the next time the manager wants the reporter to cover a story, there may be a less than enthusiastic response or, worse yet, the reporter will go out of his or her way to include arguments from opponents.

Editors have the same concerns about getting the news right as reporters. They are also responsible to the paper's management to include a wide variety of news, help prevent advertisers from public embarrassment, and make the front-page sell papers. In radio and television, the front page would be the leadoff story that is plugged in teaser ads leading up to the newscast. Closer to the EMS manager's perspective, the editor is also the person who decides which reporter is assigned to each story, or even if the story is covered at all. Finally, depending on the size of the media outlet, the editor singly or as part of a group writes editorials expressing the opinion and voice of the paper or station. No matter what positive facts have been reported, an editorial can spell doom for an EMS manager's message. For these reasons, a good relationship with editors is another must-have for EMS managers.

Columnists offer a mix of reporting and opinion in their views of whatever subject has struck their fancy. Because they have a standing space to fill every day of publication—be it daily, weekly, monthly, and so on—having a good relationship with a columnist can increase the chance of having your message heard. Because columnists are allowed to express their own opinions, they are not duty bound to look at more than just your side of the story. Cultivating good relationships with columnists can help you spread your message using the voice local people already know, like, and trust.

You should treat the press as its own entity, separate from your other audiences. In some ways, the press is a partner, helping you reach your audiences. In other ways, it can almost take on the role of a stakeholder if its investigations and reporting cause changes to your agency. Which audience your local press fits into depends in large part on how well you conduct your outreach to them.

As you gather contact information on area media, do not limit yourself to local papers and stations. Look outside your community for radio and television stations that are not located in town but are still popular with local people. Look for all the newspapers that serve your area, especially the nearest metropolitan daily. These papers are constantly seeking news from surrounding areas to help them build circulation outside their metro base.

CHAPTER REVIEW

Summary

Identifying and collecting contact information on all your potential audiences can seem a daunting task, but it is well worth the effort. One of the worst things that can happen to any manger is to be surprised by someone they do not know demanding information. If the request is from an unidentified stakeholder, the perils can be much greater than a citizen complaint.

Identifying and cataloging everyone you may need to contact, or answer to, makes the next steps easier. When the need to communicate a message arises, you already have a prepared list of who needs to hear it and how to reach them. This saves time, ensures complete coverage, and makes your agency look like a smooth-running operation.

WHAT WOULD YOU DO? Reflection

As Les reviewed his mail and email inbox, he began to sort the contents into four groups: stakeholders, partners, targeted public groups, and personnel. He gave press contacts a place of their own. By separating the message senders into groups, it clearly defined what kind of information each individual would need or be interested in. Within each group, he then separated out messages based on whether they were informing him or requesting information from him. Those requesting information were examined for potential to become the basis of new information or education campaigns.

Les built a database of contact information that could be searched by name or organization. Individual addresses, phone numbers, and email addresses were easily retrieved when he needed to send a message to a particular person or organization.

Within his groups, he also created bulk-email address files to save time when he had to send the same message to multiple people. For example, one bulk email address file would let him send an email to every employee with a single click. Another bulk address file gave him access to every elected official on his agency's board of commissioners.

As new names and organizations are identified by a search or receipt of a message from them, they can easily be added into the appropriate places in Les's database.

Review Questions

1. Give at least three immediate advantages to creating a robust catalog of previously identified audiences.
2. Into what four broad groups are audiences categorized?
3. Give two examples of stakeholders at the national, state, and local level.
4. Give at least five examples of partners.
5. What is the difference between reporters, editors, and columnists?
6. Who are targeted audience groups? Give an example.

References

Mitterer, Dennis.(2015) EMS Finance, Upper Saddle River, New Jersey: Pearson Education.

Key Terms

personnel Agency staff members at all levels and in all job categories, regardless of whether or not they are compensated financially for their efforts.

targeted public groups Specific groups identified by their common needs, interests, or goals.

CHAPTER 5

Categorizing Messages by Type and Audience

Objectives

After reading this chapter, the student should be able to:

5.1 Recognize the different types of incoming and outgoing messaging needs in an EMS agency.
5.2 Match message topics and content with targeted audiences.
5.3 Recognize, create, and capitalize on opportunities to inform and educate different audiences.

Overview

This title identifies and offers examples of the informational and educational components that work together to form a comprehensive public relations plan. Capitalizing on successful strategies used in marketing and advertising, it explains the reasons why public information and education are necessary for gaining and holding the public trust.

Key Terms

capital improvement fund	facilities	newsworthy
	fact sheet	noteworthy

You need to be able to categorize your different audiences according to what they mean to your agency. *Courtesy of Jeffrey T. Lindsey, Ph.D.*

Les Phillips has created a way to categorize all his different audiences according to

what they mean to his agency. In the process of doing this, he realized that each audience also varies in the type of information they seek from him, or in the type of message he would want to send to them. He begins to wonder if he might be able to streamline his messaging and information workload by identifying them by type.

Questions

1. Can Les create a means to identify incoming and outgoing messages by type?
2. Can this categorization work in correlation with his identified audiences?
3. Can he create a streamlined means of accessing information when needed?

■ INTRODUCTION

Categorizing audiences by type provides a means of easily identifying what role any contact plays in the operation of any EMS agency. When you know what stakeholders do, you can take the next logical step toward knowing what kind of information they want. It also helps guide you toward developing messaging that can specifically address a need you have to deliver information in language that the stakeholder group will understand.

However, what is each audience interested in knowing? Part of the answer lies in the questions they ask. Another part of the answer lies in the information and educational messages the EMS manager distributes. Answering questions is a reactive activity, offering less control over what information is disseminated. Offering information and education is a proactive activ-

ity that lets the EMS manager both to tell the facts he or she deems important and to place them into the best context for the agency.

An encyclopedic knowledge of the agency would be nice to have. Not all managers are so well equipped. Nor can any new manager be expected to possess such total recall. This is why some documented research into the agency and categorization of the information are required. Institutional information is memorialized to prevent loss with turnover. In addition, identifying information by type will allow any EMS manager to easily connect the right message to the right audience.

For the purposes of public information and education work, content of agency messages can be categorized into five areas:

- System component identification
- System design

* Agency financing
* Special programs
* Agency accomplishments

Stakeholders will be interested in financing and system design. Partners will be asked to help with special programs. Accomplishments are prime messages to send to all appropriate audiences.

■ SYSTEM COMPONENT IDENTIFICATION

An EMS agency is the sum of lots of individual parts. What the public sees driving down the road is only the public interface of the agency. The ambulance or department vehicle and its occupants would not be there without an entire system behind the scenes supporting their activities. As an EMS manager looking to inform and educate your audiences, you need to be able to identify and explain each component thoroughly and accurately, no matter the audience with which you are communicating. What are these components, who wants to know about them, and who do you want to inform about them?

FACILITIES

Facilities include any structures the agency uses to house apparatus, personnel, equipment, classrooms, and administrative offices. The stakeholders who control agency budgets want to get the most for their money. Partners may want to share space, especially for joint training operations. Public groups may ask to use meeting and classroom space for their own purposes, such as scout meetings and neighborhood association meetings. In many rural parts of the United States, the local fire and EMS station is also the town's community center where everything from weddings to birthdays to memorial services takes place.

Create a database on all your agency's facilities, and include the following:

* Location
* Staffing hours (if applicable)
* Emergency resources available
* Contact information
* Services offered to the public such as blood pressure checks
* Meeting space available for groups
* Regularly scheduled public meetings
* Photos (see Figure 5.1)

Compile this information for stakeholders, partners, targeted public groups, and the press. Questions from any group can be easily answered by doing a quick search. For example, a teacher calls with a request for her fourth-grade class to tour a local station. You go to the database and send her complete information about Station 5, just a few blocks from the school.

EQUIPMENT FACT SHEETS

Most of what people know about EMS is what they see on television and in the movies. They will ask questions like, among others, "Do you have and use the Jaws of Life?" and "Do your medics use paddles to shock cardiac patients like the old reruns on TV?" They will also want to know, in addition to what many EMS providers would consider to be their routine daily-use equipment, if your agency has the equipment and training to perform heavy rescue, water rescue, high-angle and low-angle rope rescue, technician-level hazardous materials mitigation, and other highly specialized operations.

Develop a **fact sheet** that includes photos for each piece of specialized equipment your agency carries as well as the following:

* Proper and generally accepted nicknames or slang terms
* Original cost, lifespan, and estimated replacement cost

Figure 5.1 ■ Create a database on all your agency's facilities and include photos. *Courtesy of Jeffrey T. Lindsey, Ph.D.*

- Number of devices and apparatus/stations where they are located
- Capabilities and uses
- When the equipment was used locally in the past, especially in well-known incidents
- Initial and ongoing training required for operation
- Number and percentage of agency personnel trained to operate/use
- Interesting physical attributes (size, weight, etc.)

This fact sheet becomes a handy reference with multiple uses with different audiences.

When stakeholders with budget authority are asked to fund replacement equipment, a well-ordered and informative fact sheet will demonstrate exactly how the tool is used and needed for the agency to do its work.

When the press calls for more information about a motor vehicle accident where a patient was extricated using hydraulic power tools, a fact sheet for those tools saves you and the reporter time and gives the reporter accurate information.

When responders give a presentation on recognizing heart attack and stroke symptoms in a senior community, they can show the cardiac monitoring equipment carried in the fleet and can hand out fact sheets telling all about it. This also may help save lives by inspiring confidence among residents to call 9-1-1 rather than try to get themselves to the hospital.

APPARATUS FACT SHEETS

Fire-based EMS agencies are used to having the public flock to the fire trucks, often while ignoring the medic units and ambulances, although those vehicles are every bit as necessary a component of an EMS agency's system. As with specialty equipment, create fact sheets that include photos for all your agency's response vehicles:

* Make, model, year
* Type of response unit
* Whether used for patient transport or not
* Location where stationed
* Typical staffing and responder certifications
* Initial and estimated replacement cost
* Estimated lifespan
* Types of calls used for
* Annual call volume
* Equipment carried

EMS vehicle fact sheets offer an opportunity to inform and educate audiences on a subject that is often overlooked. Financial stakeholders want to know how funds are used. Regulatory stakeholders are interested in knowing if the vehicle, staff, and equipment fall within legal constraints. EMS managers want the public to know the capabilities of their staff and vehicles and thus to prompt more timely calls for emergency medical help.

HOW TO IDENTIFY PERSONNEL

Personnel are the core of any organization. Trained hands and skilled technicians turn lifeless vehicles and equipment into instruments that save lives. The public is curious who these "heroes" are. The press is always looking for a great hero story. Partners want to learn more about who they work with. Stakeholders need to know they have quality people working under their jurisdiction.

How you choose to create a personnel identification document is up to you. Without exposing confidential information, for each member it should at least include the following:

* Name and job title
* Certifications(s) and/or licensure
* Time in the agency
* Time in the industry, if different
* Work location

* Awards and recognition
* Links to press reports featuring the person

Once you have collected the information, you may choose to organize and present it in different ways, depending on its intended audience. For example, for stakeholders you may want to organize by certification level; for public and press audiences, you might organize it alphabetically; for personnel use, the information can be presented as a traditional organizational chart showing where each person fits into the agency's hierarchy and geographic distribution.

LEVELS OF SERVICE

Fire-based advanced life support (ALS), non-transporting basic life support (BLS), hospital-based ALS, rescue squad: What do these all mean? Service levels are described within the industry using jargon that is well-known internally but can be meaningless to anyone outside the agency.

Fire departments put out fires. Police departments arrest criminals. The street department maintains the roads. What does an EMS agency do? Your service levels identify the scope of practice and types of medical emergencies your agency is licensed, trained, and equipped to handle. Service levels constitute the umbrella under which your various audiences understand what you do.

Develop single-page fact sheets that describe what types of services you provide in plain language. Explain what BLS services means. Compare and contrast to ALS-level services. If your agency does not provide ALS-level service, define it anyway, identify who does provide that level of care in your area, and explain how yours and this other agency work together. Use the same concept if you use another agency or company to transport patients. People want to know why "two ambulances" were sent.

If you are a fire-based EMS system, explain how the fire, rescue, and EMS services are provided by the different personnel and apparatus in each station. Again, people don't understand why a fire truck came to their trauma call or heart attack unless you explain the shared responsibilities in a fire-based EMS system. Distribute this information to all responders so they can assist with this public education component in real time.

Best Practice

Louisville Metro Emergency Medical Services (LMEMS)

Louisville Metro Emergency Medical Services (LMEMS) provides 24-hour-a-day, 911 emergency medical care throughout the Louisville, KY Metro area. Medically focused and data-driven, LMEMS is committed to the development of the latest advances in basic and advanced life support patient care. Utilizing a comprehensive approach to education, training, technology and research, the goal of LMEMS is to provide a "Best-Practice" model for EMS to those whose visit, reside and work in Louisville Metro.

LMEMS is built upon the strong foundations of the former Jefferson County and Louisville Fire Department EMS systems. Providing a broad spectrum of community-based outreach programs in stroke, cardiovascular disease, and accident prevention, LMEMS works to promote wider public use of cardiopulmonary resuscitation (CPR) and defibrillation. LMEMS website touts a number of public information and education programs to inform their residents and visitors.

Here are a couple of sample press releases found on their website with press releases.

December 9, 2009 Bluecoats luncheon honors public safety workers

More than 20 public safety workers were honored Wednesday during the annual BlueCoats luncheon, most of them for their response to a July house fire that killed six people.

October 5, 2009 Bellarmine University Student Group Will Provide Emergency Services at Campus Events

Bellarmine University and Louisville Metro EMS announced today the creation of the new Bellarmine Emergency Response Team, known as BERT, a team of specially trained student emergency medical responders for the university campus.

September 29, 2009 Middle Schoolers Get CPR Training

Beginning this week, about 1,400 Jefferson County seventh-graders at six schools will get a one-time, 20-minute CPR training. They'll be able to take home a kit that includes an inflatable practice dummy, a booklet, and an instructional DVD to teach parents and neighbors.

Source: www.louisvilleky.gov/ems

■ SYSTEM DESIGN

System design issues involve combining system components with agency policies and procedures to do the emergency medical treatment and transportation work the EMS agency exists to provide. It takes more than facilities, equipment, apparatus, and personnel to provide emergency medical services. The system design links together all the components to provide the desired levels of service to the community.

What the EMS system design elements are and how they work together may be where the community and press are misinformed or uninformed. All they know is that help arrives when they call 9-1-1. Hopefully, the help is timely, accurate, and performed with a great deal of care.

Dividing the system design into four basic elements offers the EMS manager a chance to define and describe each individually. The four include the public safety access point, response procedures, agency capabilities, and agency operations. With this understanding, the manager can then combine them as needed to answer questions or develop public information and educational materials.

WHEN 9-1-1 IS CALLED

An elderly woman's husband is pale, short of breath, and clutching his chest. A mother watches her child take a bad tumble on his bicycle and not get up out of the street. A pedestrian waiting for the walk light at a street corner sees a city bus strike someone running out from between parked cars midblock. They are all going to have the same reaction: frantically dial 9-1-1 for help.

What they do not know about what happens next often leads to needless frustration, anxiety, and irritation at their local emergency services. Callers believe that the call taker is wasting their time asking so many questions rather than sending help. What they do not realize is how work is shared—or multitasked—so that resources are being dispatched during, not after, the interview. Updates are sent to responding units as more information becomes available through the interview process, or from subsequent calls on incidents being reported by multiple callers.

Visit your agency's dispatch center. Depending on the size of your area, it can range from a single person in your agency, to one or two people in an office, to a comprehensive

public safety access point (PSAP) that handles incoming calls and radio traffic for multiple law enforcement, fire, and EMS agencies. Learn what happens in your jurisdiction when someone makes a call to the PSAP, then create a flowchart for public distribution that includes the following:

* Who answers the call?
* If used, how does the enhanced 9-1-1 information get to the call taker?
* What kind of questions get asked of the caller?
* Is the call taker sending this information to a radio dispatcher, or multitasking the job by themselves?
* How are the responding units contacted and dispatched?
* How do the PSAP and responding units keep each other updated on the call?

If your PSAP is operated by an outside company or government agency, it is an important partner with just as much vested interest as much as you are in good public information and education. Enlist their help in preparing the document for public consumption. Consider also allowing (or even requiring) PSAP personnel and EMS responders to share shifts with each other. Responders will learn more about how the PSAP works and what they can do to improve communications. PSAP personnel will see firsthand what happens in the field and the types of environments to which they are sending responders. With greater knowledge comes a better working relationship because both groups will have more understanding and respect for each other's jobs.

Side Bar

OnStar is a system predominantly installed in General Motors vehicles. The company has made a concerted effort to partner with EMS, fire, and PSAP agencies. In turn the agencies have promoted this service to the general public. OnStar provides assistance to the public safety agencies to promote this service. When a vehicle is involved in a vehicle crash, the OnStar operator is notified and in turn requests a response to the scene of the incident by contacting the designated PSAP. OnStar has done a great job of partnering and marketing its service by working with all the constituents involved.

RESPONSE PROCEDURES

Response procedures define how system components work together to respond to the emergency call. Based on the given circumstances, selected apparatus carrying certain equipment from selected facilities respond in emergency or nonemergency fashion, carrying sufficient numbers of personnel trained at the appropriate level to successfully mitigate the problem to be faced.

How this all comes to be is the result of years of planning, experimenting, run reviews, and response to changes in population, call type, and jurisdictions. Whether called a response menu, a pick list, or some other title, documenting response procedures provides valuable information to a number of audiences.

Budgetary stakeholders are concerned about providing sufficient resources, but also want to be sure they are not being wasted. Regulatory stakeholders need to know that the appropriate resources are being sent to each emergency call. PSAP partners need a defined response menu that matches resources to calls. EMS responders want to know what they will get if for multiple calls or multiple-patient calls they call for additional resources. The public wants to know why two ambulances or a fire truck are on scene, and why so many people are crammed into their living room.

For stakeholders, create a list of resources dispatched based on call type. Differenti-

ate ALS versus BLS, medical versus trauma, single-patient versus mass-casualty incidents. For working with response partners and your own responders, distribute a comprehensive list of the response packages on file at the PSAP. Create fact sheets for the public that contain examples of frequently run calls. (See Figure 5.2.) Include explanations of the role of each response unit, unit personnel from your agency, and any partners involved with the goal of answering the common "Why is this truck at my house?" or "Why are so many people here?"

AGENCY CAPABILITIES

EMS is an all-hazards business. How many of those hazards an agency can handle on its own and which ones require additional outside resources is of much interest to different audiences. Does the agency provide ALS and BLS services, or is it BLS only? Are both responders on a unit trained to the same level, or does the agency run a mixed crew? How many calls can the agency run simultaneously?

What type of special services is the agency capable of handling? Does it have the resources, equipment, and trained personnel to decontaminate patients, enter hazardous material warm or hot zones, perform specialty rescue procedures?

Even more so than EMS, your PSAP partner is an all-hazards agency. No matter what comes in over the phone or radio, the PSAP partner has to find someone to send out and mitigate the problem. Beginning with your response procedures, your PSAP partner needs to know what types of calls your agency is capable of handling and when to look somewhere else for help. Businesses and industries locating or expanding in your community need to know if local resources are adequate to address any emergency that may occur with their products or facilities. Industrial plants may become strategic partners using their

FIGURE 5.2 ■ You should be able to explain the role of each response unit, unit personnel from your agency, and any partners with the goal of answering the common questions, "Why is this truck at my house?" or "Why are so many people here?" *Courtesy of Ed Mund.*

in-house resources and personnel to assist the local EMS agency coming onto their property.

A simple listing of capabilities begins with what your daily staffing can handle with its apparatus, equipment, training, and staffing. Additional capabilities can be added by title with a short paragraph explaining what types of incidents can be managed, along with information on how to access these resources. Distribute this information to strategic partners to streamline the call-up process when the emergency occurs.

■ AGENCY FINANCING

Whether funded by tax dollars, corporate budgets, or donations, an EMS agency cannot do its job without money in the bank—although

to some small, nonprofit volunteer groups, it may seem they actually do. Just like fuel makes the vehicles move, money primes the pump to makes things happen. Where that money comes from and how it is spent is a major concern to stakeholders with budget authority, agency administrators who spend the money, and personnel who earn their income from the agency. Equally concerned are those who are the source of the money, be they taxpayers, customers, insurance companies, or corporate boards.

Although the EMS manager does not need to know every line item in the budget, he or she should have a good working knowledge of the agency's income and expense streams. Can each source of income be identified? Can where each income stream fits into the agency's day-to-day operations and long-term financial planning be discussed intelligently?

Armed with this knowledge, the EMS manager can start to identify information related to the agency's income and expenses, and can place it into some broad categories: ongoing sources of income and expenses, special sources of income and expenses, and capital improvement funds. When questions come in or information needs to be disseminated, the manager has instant access to correct numbers and processes.

ONGOING SOURCES OF INCOME AND EXPENSES

Ongoing sources of income and expenses are commonly known as the agency's operating budget. The income comprises funds that can be counted on to come in from whatever source, and are relied upon to cover the costs of day-to-day agency operations. In a publicly funded agency, the ongoing income is the amount of taxpayer dollars that will legally be collected and disbursed to the agency in the current fiscal year. In unincorporated jurisdictions, the income amount is fixed by law and paid to the agency upon collection. In incorporated jurisdictions, the agency's available income may be determined by an elected board or city council that is not required to disburse according to any set distribution structure. Depending on state and local laws, money may only be spent in the year it is collected, or some can be carried over into the next fiscal year.

For privately owned EMS agencies, funding comes from customers and the agency's ownership. For private nonprofits, customers, donors, and fund-raising efforts provide income. Both public and private agencies may derive a portion of their ongoing income from billings to insurance companies, Medicare, and Medicaid.

Although sources of money may be different, all agencies determine how the available dollars are spent in the budgeting process. Typically, budgets are drawn up by agency leadership, then submitted to an elected or appointed board for approval, depending on the agency's governance structure. The goal is to have anticipated expenses not exceed available income for daily operations.

An easy way for the EMS manager to understand and disseminate operating budget information is to stick to large, understandable categories such as facilities, fuel, vehicle maintenance, wages, benefits, equipment, supplies, training, and so on. Visual representations are excellent ways to deliver this information. Pie charts easily convey from where income is derived and how income and expenses compare relative to the various categories.

SPECIAL SOURCES OF INCOME AND EXPENSES

In addition to the operating income and expenses, several other avenues of funding are available and may be in use by your agency. What differentiates these funding sources from operating income may be their duration, source, or specifically targeted objectives.

Grants are popular sources of additional income because they provide money for a special purpose in what is usually a one-time offer. Because of their single distribution and targeted use, grant funds are not recommended for operating costs. They are most often used to purchase equipment, training, and other resources the agency has not been able to afford from its operating budget. Internet searches and talking to neighboring agency managers are good ways to find what is available at any given time.

Donations are another special source of income. The funds may be sought from a corporate or humanitarian source by the agency management, much like writing a grant proposal. Other donations come from memorial contributions as members of the community use contributions from loved ones and life insurance policies to thank their local EMS agency for a job well done. Depending on the size of the donation and any restrictions placed on the funds by the donor, this income may be placed into the operating account or used like a grant to purchase something not otherwise affordable in the operating budget.

Long-term loans offer a means of purchasing necessary big-ticket items that would never otherwise be possible using available operating funds. An agency could never afford to buy a new medic unit that costs as much as an agency's entire monthly budget. Nevertheless, that agency could afford the monthly payments on a loan to purchase the unit. The same holds true for even bigger-ticket items, like a new station to replace one that is no longer serviceable, or to expand coverage for new response requirements.

Rather than approach a bank, publicly funded agencies use voter-approved funding measures as a form of long-term loan. Voters are asked in an election to approve increasing their taxes for a certain period in order to raise a predetermined amount of money. Just like a loan or grant funding, because this funding stream has a time limit, agencies use these measures to fund large purchases, not ongoing operations.

When explaining loans or voter-approved measures to various audiences, it is a good idea also to include the agency's operating budget information. It will show how the loan payment is funded on the expenses side, and clearly show how the operating income side would never have produced enough to meet the challenge on its own.

CAPITAL IMPROVEMENT FUNDS

Another means of generating the income needed for large cash purchases is to set aside money every year from the operating account to improve or build or acquire new system components with an expected usage life of more than 1 year in a **capital improvement fund**. Let us say the average lifespan of a medic unit is 10 years before it needs to be replaced. If 10 percent of the cost of a new unit is placed into a capital improvement fund every year, by the tenth year the fund will cover the cost of a new unit.

When funding is tight, capital improvement funds are hard to justify to budget stakeholders or the tax-paying public. Sometimes all they see is the pool of money sitting untouched as a line item in the budget. They need to be educated on how this funding mechanism saves money in the end by preventing the need for loans and ensures the future operations of the agency. Get help from the agency's budget writers, facilities managers, and vehicle experts to help explain how and why this is a wiser use of the money rather than dropping it back into the operating fund.

Questions and issues over funding are some of the most common interactions the EMS manager will have with various audiences. People may not know how EMS services are provided, but they all understand the value of a dollar—especially if it is their dollar being spent by someone other than themselves. Creating simple yet explanatory methods of showing how every dollar is accounted for will help stop questions and resolve arguments. Being able to prove good stewardship of the funds entrusted to the agency will also pay dividends when submitting grant requests, applying for a loan, or asking voters for more of their tax dollars.

■ SPECIAL PROGRAMS ────────

EMS agencies are well-known for going out into their communities to improve quality of life for the residents. Alone or with partners, EMS agencies have a long history of doing much more than responding to calls for help. These outreach efforts pay dividends as ways to inform and educate the public on a wide range of health-related topics. They can also generate a positive public perception of the agency. Working with partners offers all participants an opportunity to get to know each other's staff, learn what each partner's mandates and priorities are, and understand how each partner operates.

NONEMERGENCY PROGRAMS

EMS and fire stations are visited every day by local people looking to get their blood pressure checked. Physicians recommend going to their neighborhood station for accurate readings to help track the progress of disease processes, or to measure the effectiveness of a treatment regimen. While at the station, the resident should be exposed to printed information and educational materials in the lobby. There they should be engaged with professional, caring responders who can take the time to answer questions and promote the agency's public information goals. Free community health care along with a dose of information and education create a combination no agency should pass up.

In communities where budgets, scope-of-practice laws, and responder time permit, community outreach wellness programs have taken root. With permission from the patient, EMS responders visit known shut-ins who have medical conditions and trouble accessing outside medical assistance. These encounters improve the patient's quality of life while at the same time reducing the agency's emergency call volume. While checking up on the patient, responders can survey the scene and help educate the patient on ways to improve their living conditions and overall health.

COMMUNITY PARTNERSHIPS

Community partnerships offer EMS agencies opportunities to conduct public information and education programs on a larger scale than they could do by themselves. Obvious choices to partner with are other public safety agencies such as law enforcement and the fire department. Advocacy groups that promote public health and safety choices have much in common with an EMS agency's goal to reduce pain and suffering. Other choices could include scout troops, schools, community centers, neighborhood associations, and groups that provide the social services safety net in the community.

Health fairs are a popular way for public service agencies to inform and educate the public. A multi-agency effort offers a way to build a larger event with multiple facets that draws larger numbers of people than a single-focused event would. The EMS agency can teach about injury prevention, bicycle helmets, and a wide variety of other healthy living skills for kids and adults. Law enforcement can teach how to properly select and install child seats in cars. The fire department can show the value of smoke and carbon monoxide detectors and conduct fire extinguisher classes.

Some towns wrap all these events around a community picnic sponsored by local businesses and make an annual daylong celebration. Attendees go home fed, educated, and with a positive image of all their local public service agencies.

Public addresses in schools are another good way to reach out to children and teens with injury prevention messages. For all ages, it is another opportunity to promote bicycle helmet use. For smaller kids, develop programs to help prevent Halloween hazards, engage families in injury prevention efforts, and make children aware that they are not invulnerable. Teenagers are focusing on driving and what to do with the rest of their lives, so you can offer an existing or your own outreach program on safe driving. Develop materials that inform, educate, and potentially recruit the next generation of EMS workers.

Age-appropriate educational programs also work well in nursing homes and community association meetings. Topics such as fall prevention, disaster preparedness, group CPR, heart health, and recognizing the signs of heart attack and stroke are within the scope of an EMS agency's community coverage. Do not hesitate to do a little recruiting when the opportunity arises. Some agencies recruit drivers from young retirees looking to do something community minded. Volunteer agencies find that community groups are excellent sources of future responders. All it takes is the right information presented to the right person at the right moment to spark interest.

Some EMS agencies partner with local social services agencies in a nontraditional way to serve the public. People who are destitute, homeless, have addictions, or suffer from physical and mental illnesses can strain prehospital and hospital resources in a community. Working together, EMS agencies can help identify the people who need help and get them to the correct social services agency for care. The person's long-term needs can be better addressed there rather than in a hospital emergency department, and the EMS agency reduces its run volume by helping place frequent service users into a better environment. The partnerships between agencies are strengthened, and all see their public image improved.

PUBLIC SAFETY CLASSES

Rather than take classes to an outside venue, sometimes it is easier to offer citizen CPR classes in a more controlled environment with all the teaching tools and equipment handy. EMS agencies can utilize their own training facilities and staff to provide public safety classes for free or for a fee. Other classes may include fall prevention, heart attack and stroke recognition, and basic first aid. Getting people into your facilities is another chance to inform and educate them on a wide range of issues important to your agency.

■ AGENCY ACCOMPLISHMENTS ──

Accomplishments may be the easiest public information messaging to remember to do. Something great happened, some crisis was averted, a responder excelled, the agency won an award—the topics are wide ranging and can be significant to how stakeholders, partners, the public, personnel, and the press view the overall excellence of their EMS agency.

Different kinds of accomplishments have meaning to your different audiences. Stakeholders are interested in how standards have been met or exceeded and improvements to the system. The press wants facts fast on major incidents. Feature stories about responders and their patients are always welcome with the press, too. Partners who work within your system, especially the local PSAP and fellow responders, are interested in learning about and helping achieve improvements. Personnel's pride in their agency increases with every good report or story on the news.

DIFFERENTIATE NOTEWORTHY VERSUS NEWSWORTHY

The most common distribution method for announcing accomplishments is the media. However, differentiating whether something is **noteworthy** versus **newsworthy** must be done, and it occurs in two separate equations. Noteworthy is your opinion of how important the accomplishment or achievement is. A single responder passing a national certification exam is always noteworthy, but may not be deemed important enough to draft a press release. On the other hand, if an entire class of new responders pass their national certification exam with record high marks, that is both noteworthy and newsworthy in your community.

Second, not everything you think is newsworthy may meet that definition by your local media. You are focused on your agency, so any significant accomplishment is a big deal to you and everyone else in the agency. The press will balance your news against its value to readers/viewers/listeners as an entire group. The press must also balance how important your story is to its followers in comparison to the other news of the day. Do not take it personally if an accomplishment you think is monumental is ignored or receives less media play than you want.

STANDARDS MET OR EXCEEDED

Comparisons to industry and legal standards are the measures by which EMS agencies are rated. Failure to meet any comes with a price—financial, legal, lives, or jobs. Tracking performance according to accepted standards is a big part of any EMS manager's job. Is your agency meeting or exceeding industry standard or contractually obligated response times? Do cardiac arrest patients have higher survival rates in your jurisdiction than elsewhere in the state or nationally? Are your responders significantly exceeding requirements through national certifications or have additional skills been acquired?

Use the positive data generated to inform your various audiences about the excellence of the agency. Financial stakeholders are more inclined to increase support of a well-run agency. Personnel are inspired to continue to excel. Positive public opinion is always desired, especially when public agencies approach their taxpayers with a financing dilemma.

CORRECTLY REPORTING MAJOR INCIDENT FACTS

Making sure that what the press reports is in line with the public image you want of your agency requires approaching the press in a proactive rather than reactive manner. Although your natural reaction may be to run away from the press, it is in your best interest to engage the media directly.

For example, your agency is working a multiple-car accident on a freeway off-ramp. A helicopter has been airlifted to transport one critical patient. The incident commander has asked the state police to shut down the freeway traffic in order to land the helicopter near the scene. During the 10 minutes the traffic was stopped, a crash in the backup resulted in the death of another motorist. A proactive manager will go to the press on scene and explain how and why the 10-minute closure was an operational and medical necessity and offered the least risk to rescuers working on scene. A reactive manager may spend the next several days trying to explain away the press's conclusion that emergency responders caused the motorist's death by closing the freeway for no good reason.

In addition to having already established a relationship with your local media representatives, always be available with accurate information during and immediately after major incidents. Seek out the press before a story is filed and be able to answer all questions on the spot. Carry the fact sheets you have created about apparatus, personnel, equipment, and system operations so you can refer to the content in the heat of the moment or at 3:00 a.m. when your recall is not at its best.

Be sure all your personnel know to refer press questions to the commander on scene if possible, or to the agency public information officer. Remind them of their obligations under the law and agency guidelines to protect all private patient information, no matter who is asking questions. Specific agency guidelines should cover the transfer of appropriate patient information, including photographic documentation where appropriate.

The alternative will be having to react to something that has already been reported, possibly incorrectly. You will spend more time contacting each member of the media one by one than if you had been able to talk with them all at once at the scene. In addition, the public may only see or remember the initial, incorrect report. Nothing you can do at this point will change the impression of people you cannot reach.

Finally, establishing an open and partnering relationship with the press will demonstrate that you are someone they can access and trust. Having the press on your side from the outset will pay dividends on the accuracy of what is reported, the benefit of the doubt when questions come up, and some extra consideration in the noteworthy versus newsworthy decisions down the road.

MAKING MINOR ITEMS NEWSWORTHY

It is difficult to transition minor incidents from noteworthy to newsworthy. Because by definition a minor incident does not rate a lot of attention, it seems doomed from the start. The way to turn something minor into something newsworthy is to find a hook—something about the item that makes it compelling.

For example, having an EMT go to school and become a paramedic is not, in and of itself, a big story. This happens every day around the county. However, what if a responder you hired has a personal story behind her drive to work in emergency medicine? She's a mother who almost killed her choking child quite innocently by not knowing what to do and, in fact, doing all the wrong things. Timely arrival by EMS saved the child in spite of her efforts. Her child's survival has inspired her to never want to feel helpless around her children again, and to dedicate her life to helping others. Her honesty and dedication have turned your minor item into a feature story that will run in the local

media and get picked up by her hometown paper in another state. Readers will feel good about her and about your agency for having the good sense to hire her.

Similar hooks can be found to turn other seemingly minor items into positive press. Perhaps your agency has met a new state requirement. The hook is that you are the first agency to do so and accomplished it in half the time predicted by the state.

Little things happen more frequently than big things. Look at them all with an eye for turning them into an opportunity to present your agency in a positive light. Then arrange for the media and the appropriate members of your agency to get the story reported.

RECOGNIZING ACHIEVEMENT

Nothing rewards and inspires people more than validation. Somebody noticed. Somebody cared. Somebody recognizes who I am or what I did. Turn this validation into informational and educational moments for the agency, too. The press loves to print feature stories that add emotion and depth to the facts of a news story. Engage the press to write about a recently completed project. Include any partners and all personnel who took part in turning the project idea into reality.

Individual and group training that enhances the agency's service levels is newsworthy. Maybe two responders attend training to become rope rescue instructors. They come back, secure the equipment needed, and train the rest of your agency's responders. Your agency now has a new level of service to offer that will be of great interest to your stakeholders, partners, and the public.

EMS, fire, and police responders are often called heroes in the press and seen that way in the public eye. Once in a while, significant performance on a call lives up to the labels and expectations. Pulling the driver from a burning car, delivering twins in the back of the medic unit, rescuing a sanitation worker from a pipe 150 feet below ground— these are all individual or group achievements that are newsworthy. Be sure accurate information is given to the press as soon as possible.

These are the stories that stakeholders will brag about to their friends. Responders will keep clippings in scrapbooks and use these experiences for the rest of their careers to help mentor and teach newer members. The public will learn of these accomplishments and look on their local EMS agency with pride and support.

SYSTEM IMPROVEMENTS

System improvements can be a dry subject for the public unless the improvement is something they understand, like faster response times. On the other hand, stakeholders, partners, and personnel are fully in tune with improvement efforts. Those who have participated in a specific effort will

want to know the outcome and be credited for their work.

When reporting system improvements to the public, remember that they do not have the same grasp of how your agency operates as your stakeholders do. Overcome this knowledge gap by providing additional information in language your audience will understand. Now when the target audience reads the report, you achieve two goals: (1) report on the achievement, how it was accomplished, and its significance and (2) further educate the reader about how the agency operates.

The types of improvements that could be reported include, for example, introducing systems status management to reduce response times, using innovative staffing methods to save payroll costs or improve coverage, initiating a nurse diversion phone line to reduce minor aid calls, installing computer-aided dispatch with GPS into vehicles, or adding an emergency medical dispatch system to your PSAP.

When system improvements are made, be sure to go back to all the previously created and appropriate fact sheets and make any changes so they remain up to date.

CHAPTER REVIEW

Summary

Audiences and information must be linked together. Audiences with no information have no way to help the agency, nor any reason to do so. Information stored away in files does no good if it is never used. The EMS manager may spend a lot of time on how the agency does patient care, but that actually is the job of the responders and street-level supervisors. The manager's job is to make sure everyone is working with the best information available. From stakeholders to partners to employees

and the public, getting the right information to the right place at the right time makes every audience pull in the same direction on behalf of the agency.

Anticipating the informational needs of your various audiences will allow you to prepare in advance. You will never be caught off-guard on the basics, and you will be in a position to easily and properly inform and educate anyone on any related topic.

In a similar fashion to how he categorized his audiences, Les has developed a framework for categorizing incoming and outgoing messages by type:

* System component
* System design
* Financing
* Special program
* Accomplishments

Within each category, he has created some common subcategories to further define the main thrust of the message.

Once the messages were defined by type, cross-categorizing them with the correct audience(s) became an easy task. Having already identified his targeted audiences, the category titles themselves suggest who would be most interested.

When fact sheets and news clippings were created, he does not file them away in a drawer. Les puts everything he creates on his agency's website. He turns all of his fact sheets into printable PDF files for easy retrieval and reference by himself or anyone else. The facility and apparatus sheets let anyone virtually tour the entire agency. He developed a common template for these PDF files so that when they are printed, they provide contact information for asking further questions.

Review Questions

1. Into what five areas can agency messages be categorized for the purposes of public information and education work?
2. Name at least four items you should maintain as part of your agency's facilities database.
3. What are the four basic elements into which you should divide the system design when communicating to the public?
4. Create a flowchart for public distribution of what happens in your jurisdiction when someone makes a call to the PSAP.
5. In what broad categories can you identify information related to the agency's income and expenses?
6. Give an example of a newsworthy versus a noteworthy event.

Key Terms

capital improvement fund Money set aside to improve or build or acquire new system components with a more than 1-year expected usage.

facilities Buildings utilized by the agency.

fact sheet Page containing authoritative data relative to a specific topic.

newsworthy Assumed to be interesting, significant, or usual enough to appeal to the general population.

noteworthy Interesting, significant, or unusual to individuals in a subset of the general population, but less broadly appealing than something that is newsworthy.

CHAPTER **6**

Craft the Message

Objectives

After reading this chapter, the student should be able to:

6.1 Explain what message content different audiences require.
6.2 Discuss how to write effectively for the delivery method chosen.
6.3 Describe the tools and techniques for blending data with other elements to improve messages.

Overview

This title identifies and offers examples of the informational and educational components that work together to form a comprehensive public relations plan. Capitalizing on successful strategies used in marketing and advertising, it explains the reasons why public information and education are necessary for gaining and holding the public trust.

Key Terms

boilerplate paragraph	language	sample outlines
executive summary	lead	taxpayers
feature	manual of style	testimonial
hard news	reports	

WHAT WOULD YOU DO?

The most obvious distinction is how much industry jargon versus plain-language descriptions to use to make the same point.
Courtesy of Estero Fire Rescue.

With no formal training other than a college English class, Les Phillips knows to choose his words effectively depending on who he is communicating with. The most obvious distinction is how much industry jargon to use versus using plain-language descriptions to make the same point. Les has categorized his audiences by type: stakeholders, partners, the public, and personnel. He has also listed the types of messages in which each audience is the most interested. Now he wants to create an easy reference guide to choosing the right language for delivering messages to audiences.

Questions

1. How can Les identify the different styles and languages for communications based on the intended audience?
2. How can he develop guidelines to help him include the correct details effectively?

■ INTRODUCTION

Crafting the message with the appropriate language is imperative so your audience is able to understand and respond to the material presented. In this context, **language** means what your audience wants to know, the reading level of your audience, and how the sentences and paragraphs are constructed.

When a noteworthy accomplishment will be told to the public through the mass media, it is written differently than an operational plan being submitted to a governance board.

This chapter discusses how to deliver information in a manner the reader will understand, using sources and storytelling techniques such as data, financial impacts, historical "then versus now" comparisons, trends, projections, actions taken, actions considered, testimonials, and human interest.

■ WRITE TO YOUR AUDIENCE

You are giving a tour of your station to an elementary school class. As you prepared your remarks beforehand, you carefully considered

FIGURE 6.1 ▦ You need to carefully consider your message: what words to use and what details would interest your audience. *Source: © Dr. Bryan E. Bledsoe.*

your message: what words to use and what details would interest eight-year-olds. (See Figure 6.1.) Later, while preparing remarks for an upcoming tour by paramedic students, you again carefully considered your message: what words to use and what to show that would be of interest to them.

In both cases, the event and message were the same: This is what our station looks like, and this is what we do. What was different was how the message was crafted to reach two different audiences. Eight-year-olds want to see shiny objects and colorful bandage strips. Paramedic students want to see equipment and processes.

Various audiences have different informational needs. These needs can often overlap, as noted. The EMS manager's job is to make sure the right information is presented in the correct language to each audience. Even when the essential message content remains

the same, the language used to deliver it must speak directly to the audience.

To illustrate, we will use the example of an EMS agency's process to build, equip, and staff a new station in order to keep up with increasing demands for service. When informing your audiences of the desire to add a new station and educating them on the reasons why it is needed, must cover all appropriate message categories.

STAKEHOLDERS

Adding a new station requires buy-in from the financial stakeholders who control the agency's purse strings. They want details regarding system components and how the proposal fits into and helps overall system design. Financial questions have to be answered. The initial cost of the land, building, vehicles, equipment, and supplies have to be justified. The ongoing cost for building and vehicle upkeep, equipment, supplies, and personnel will impact the agency's annual budget for years to come.

By starting with an outline that considers all message categories, it is easier to ensure all pertinent information is included.

Side Bar

Information and education to financial stakeholders regarding a new station could be outlined by message category in the following manner.

Sample: Outline of a Financial Stakeholder's Message Categories

1. System Component—in great detail
   a. Why is the new station needed?
   b. Where is the new station being proposed?
   c. Why was this location chosen?
   d. How does this impact the response area and travel-to-destination predictions?
   e. How many vehicles are involved and of what type?
   f. How will the station be equipped?
   g. What will be the numbers and certification levels of station staffing?
2. System Design—in great detail
   a. How will the station add to the agency's capabilities?
   b. How will the new station alter current response patterns?
   c. How will average response times change or improve?
   d. How will the new station improve asset value to the agency?
   e. What is the effect on the agency's collective bargaining agreement (if one is in place)?
   f. What additional capabilities will this station host (disaster response, terrorism, rescue specialties, etc.)?
3. Agency Financing—in great detail
   a. What are the initial costs, organized by type?
   b. What are the ongoing costs, organized by type?
   c. How will the initial costs be funded?
   d. How will the ongoing costs be funded in the annual operating budget?
   e. If new revenue is needed, where will it come from?
4. Special Programs—in some detail
   a. What additional community outreach and partnerships will be possible with the new facility?
   b. Can the facility be shared with strategic partners?
5. Accomplishments—probably nothing to note now, but can be reported on later after the new station is in service for a while.

For public agencies, **taxpayers** are another important stakeholder group to inform and educate. You may be asking them to support a capital funding ballot measure for the initial costs. You will also be relying at least partially on tax revenues for ongoing expenses; if the budget requires, you may have to ask taxpayers to vote on an increased tax collection in order to cover ongoing costs. Finally, your taxpayers are also your primary public audience. For these reasons, you want to keep them informed about what the agency is doing.

Your messaging to your financial stakeholders was full of details. For your taxpayers, your message is the big picture with an emphasis on proving the need.

For agencies with personnel represented by a union and employed under a collective bargaining agreement, the union local is an important stakeholder to get on board in support of the new station. Your message to the union will emphasize the increased staffing and workload leveling to be gained by adding a new station.

Side Bar

The taxpayers' message categories outline would look like this.

Sample: Outline of Taxpayer's Message Categories

1. System Component—in overview terms
   a. Why is the new station needed?
   b. Where is the new station being proposed?
   c. Why is this the best location?
   d. How will the station be staffed and equipped?
2. System Design—in detail to show proof of need
   a. How will the station add to the agency's capabilities?
   b. How will average response times improve?
   c. What is the cost-to-benefit ratio to the community and to the citizens individually?
3. Agency Financing—in detail that shows proof of cost-effective planning
   a. What are the initial costs and funding source?
   b. What are the ongoing costs and funding source?
   c. If new revenue is needed, where will it come from?
4. Special Programs—detailing the ancillary benefits to the neighborhood and community overall
   a. What additional community outreach and partnerships will be possible with the new facility?
   b. Can the facility be shared with other public or emergency services?
5. Accomplishments—projections on benefits to the community

Side Bar

The message category outline for union information and education could look like this.

Sample: Outline of Union Message Categories

1. System Component—in some detail on the facility, in great detail on the personnel issues
   a. Why is the new station needed?
   b. Where is the new station being proposed?
   c. Why was this location chosen?
   d. How many vehicles are involved and of what type?
   e. How will the station be equipped?
   f. What will be the numbers and certification levels of station staffing?
   g. How many people will be hired and in what positions?
   h. What is the hiring process?
   i. How will staff be distributed to incorporate the new station along with the existing stations?
2. System Design—in great detail on benefits to employees
   a. How will the station add to the agency's capabilities?
   b. How will the new station alter current response patterns?
   c. How will the call volume be shared among stations to reduce over- and under-use of personnel?
   d. How will average response times change or improve?
3. Agency Financing—in overview form for costs, in detail for adverse effects
   a. What are the initial costs?
   b. What are the ongoing costs?
   c. How will the initial costs be funded?
   d. How will the ongoing costs be funded in the annual operating budget?
   e. If new revenue is needed, where will it come from?

f. How will wages and benefits be protected from being adversely affected by these new costs?

4. Special Programs—in some detail
   a. What additional community outreach and partnerships are being considered in the new facility?
   b. Might the facility be shared with strategic partners?

5. Accomplishments—projections on benefits to the employees

PARTNERS

Partners are going to want to know how the new station impacts them in terms of your added capabilities and, for some, opportunities for their own use. The first and potentially most impacted partner will be your public safety access point (PSAP). Whatever system you and your PSAP use to determine which of your resources are dispatched, depending on the type of call and location, will have to be reviewed and updated to place the new station's capabilities into the system. These changes will be worked on behind the scenes, but in the meantime, the PSAP administration may be interested in other factors just out of professional curiosity. Perhaps, too, they are also considering changes to their facilities and would like to see how you made your case.

Side Bar

Your PSAP message categories outline would include these details.

Sample: Outline of PSAP Message Categories

1. System Component—in some detail
   a. Where is the new station being proposed?
   b. How many vehicles are involved and of what type?
   c. How will the station be equipped?
   d. What will the station staffing be in terms of numbers and certification levels?

2. System Design—in great detail as it relates to how the agency and the PSAP interact on a daily basis
   a. How will the station add to the agency's capabilities?
   b. How will the new station affect PSAP workload or call volume?
   c. How will average response times change or improve?

3. Agency Financing—in some detail as a model to follow
   a. What are the overall initial costs, and how are they being funded?
   b. How will the ongoing costs be funded in the annual operating budget?
   c. If new revenue is needed, where will it come from?

4. Special Programs—in brief detail on other potential uses for the building's facilities

5. Accomplishments—anticipated improvements in any category

Public Service/Allied Health Care

Other public service partners and allied health care agency partners will want to know the impact the new station has on their operations and what opportunities they may have to use the facility for their own purposes. Can the local law enforcement agency establish a satellite office to give officers space to work in their patrol districts? Will it reduce the number of mutual aid calls requested of neighboring EMS providers? Will new specialty services be available that they can call on? Will additional resources allow them to receive mutual aid from your agency in a more timely manner than from other sources? At the same time, is the facility available for meetings and training? Is there space on the property to build a landing zone for regional air medical helicopters? When filling in this message category outline for partners, be sure to include all the ways the new station will help your partnership.

Side Bar

Sample: Outline of Public Service/Allied Health Care Message Categories

1. System Component—in brief detail
   a. Where is the proposed location of the new station?
   b. How many vehicles are involved and of what type?
   c. How will the station be equipped?
   d. What will be the numbers and certification levels of station staffing?
2. System Design—in great detail as it relates to how the agency and the partners interact on a daily basis
   a. How will the station add to the agency's capabilities?
   b. How will the new station alter current dispatch and response patterns?
   c. How will average response times change or improve?
   d. How will the call volume be shared among stations to reduce overuse of mutual aid?
   e. What additional mutual aid resources will be available?
   f. How will average response times change or improve?
3. Agency Financing—in brief detail
   a. What are the overall initial costs, and how are they being funded?
   b. How will the ongoing costs be funded in the annual operating budget?
4. Special Programs—in great detail
   a. How can partners use the facilities?
   b. Can partners co-locate response, training, or other resources at this station?
   c. What multi-agency and cooperative training opportunities will exist?
5. Accomplishments—projected improvements in any category

THE PUBLIC

For a publicly owned and funded agency, the taxpayers and the public are essentially the same stakeholders group. However, not all members of the community pay taxes, so they do not see the direct financial hit on their budget. As an example, renters do not directly pay property tax and so they are usually unaware of how much tax levied against property owners supports public services. Because of this, the outline of message categories for the general public will be very similar to, but not the same as, the one for taxpayers. Non-publicly owned agencies do not rely on the public for tax funds, but they have the same need to inform and educate their customers and cultivate goodwill in their communities. The outline of public message categories presents an overview of the agency, its needs, and how the new station will benefit the public.

Side Bar

Sample: Outline of Public Message Categories

1. System Component—in overview terms
   a. Why is the new station needed?
   b. Where is the proposed location of the new station?
   c. Why is this the best location?
   d. How will the station be staffed and equipped?
2. System Design—in overview terms to paint a positive picture of this action
   a. How will the station add to the agency's capabilities to answer anyone's "What's in it for me?" questions?
   b. How will average response times improve, and what does that mean to the average citizen?
3. Agency Financing—in overview form
   a. What are the initial costs and funding source?
   b. If new revenue is needed, where will it come from?

4. Special Programs—again, answering the "What's in it for me" question by detailing the ancillary benefits to the neighborhood and community overall
   a. What additional community outreach and partnerships will be possible with the new facility?
   b. How can community groups use the facility for meetings, classes, voting?
   c. What will staff do in and for the community from this station?
   d. What kind of groups and activities have already shown an interest?
5. Accomplishments—projections on benefits to the community

PERSONNEL

Personnel need to be informed and educated on two different aspects of the new facility. First, they will want to know how the new station affects them personally. For this, the outline offered for the union is a good start. However, your personnel are also the public face of your agency. They are ambassadors working on your behalf to help spread information to the community. As such, they need to know as much as your stakeholders. A message categories outline that is a hybrid of information sent to financial stakeholders and the union would fully educate personnel to cover all their needs.

Side Bar

Sample: Outline of Personnel Message Categories

1. System Component—in great detail
   a. Why is the new station needed?
   b. Where is the proposed location of the new station?
   c. Why was this location chosen?
   d. How many vehicles are involved and of what type?
   e. How will the station be equipped?
   f. What will the station staffing be in terms of numbers and certification levels?
   g. How many people will be hired and in what positions?
   h. What is the hiring/recruiting process?
   i. How will staff be distributed to incorporate the new station along with the existing stations?
2. System Design—in great detail on benefits to personnel
   a. How will the station add to the agency's capabilities?
   b. How will the new station alter current response patterns?
   c. How will the call volume be shared among stations to reduce over- and under-use of personnel?
   d. How will average response times change or improve?
3. Agency Financing—in great detail
   a. What are the initial costs, organized by major categories?
   b. What are the ongoing costs, organized by major categories?
   c. How will the initial costs be funded?
   d. How will the ongoing costs be funded in the annual operating budget?
   e. If new revenue is needed, where will it come from?
   f. How will wages and benefits be protected from being adversely affected by these new costs?
4. Special Programs—in great detail
   a. What additional community outreach and partnerships will be possible with the new facility?
   b. How can community groups use the facility for meetings, classes, voting?
   c. What will staff do in and for the community from this station?
   d. What kind of groups and activities have already shown an interest?
5. Accomplishments—projections based on past performance at other stations

■ WRITING TO THE MEDIUM ——————

Sample outlines are a great tool with which to begin any writing project. The outline can contain the same content, no matter what type of medium you plan to use. However, how you write—the words and sentence structure you use—varies according to the way the words will be presented. One example is the difference between writing sentences to be read to yourself versus writing sentences to be read aloud. When reading quietly to yourself, there is no need to make obvious breathing stops. Sentences can be longer, with more elaborate arguments constructed into a single sentence. Turning your outline into effective prose requires paying attention to the intended medium as well as the intended audience.

REPORTS

Reports are the long-form version of the outline, with room to include every detail as you expand the outline into a complete exploration of the subject at hand. Some people can be intimidated by the prospect of all that writing. That is where having a good outline at the start really helps. Outlines can be written as memory triggers, reminding you of what you want to say on each topic area. Alternatively, outlines can be written in the form of questions. As you answer each question in the outline, you fill in all the details you want to get into the report. The more thorough the answers, the more thorough the report.

Reports often contain an **executive summary** at the beginning. This is where you make your most important points, or stress your strongest reasons for disseminating this information. Time-challenged readers want to use this section to understand your salient points. If they need to take any action, some may decide what to do based only on the executive summary. If questions persist, they have the entire report to get further details.

For others, if your intent is to inform and educate them, the executive summary will present your message. The rest of the report will further educate readers on the subject at hand and show how you arrived at your conclusions.

Reports serve as historical records. Although the executive summary may contain some opinion as you express how and why you reached the offered conclusions, the balance of the report should be as literally factual as possible. Paint a black-and-white picture, with no shades of gray that are not introduced by the nature of the subject: This is what it is; that is what it is not.

Use a **manual of style** to help you retain consistency on spellings, punctuation, word usage, footnote indications, bibliographies, and other common writing methods. To ensure clarity, have someone who is less familiar with the subject read the report prior to distribution.

ORAL PRESENTATIONS

Oral presentations are less formally structured than written reports, but no less dependent on having all necessary facts correct and in place. Due to the difference in how the information is presented, preparation of the material varies.

For a stand-alone speech with no visual aids, look at your outline, then write the words of the speech as if you were talking to someone on the phone. Keep the sentences short enough to say them without running out of breath. Although contractions are not generally used in formal writing, it is okay to use them in the text of the speech. In reality, even if you write the speech in full words, you will likely use contractions when doing the verbal presentation. It is how we speak.

When you have the speech written, practice it by reading it aloud. (See Figure 6.2.) Do not just read it to yourself, but actually speak and project the words out loud. You can skim over awkward word combinations in your

FIGURE 6.2 ■ When you have the speech written, practice it by reading it aloud. *Courtesy of Jeffrey T. Lindsey, Ph.D.*

mind, but when actually reading aloud, they will trip you up. This practice is your chance to fix clunky sounds, substitute better-sounding words, and smooth out the tempo of the speech.

Practice from the full text until you can give the speech from the outline only. On the day of the speech, use the outline to trigger your memory while you speak to the audience. You can have the full text there if it makes you more comfortable, but try to work from the outline to avoid the temptation to read the text rather than speak to your audience.

Speeches generally give you only a short time to inform your audience. If your goal is to also educate them with additional details, there are two methods you can use even with limited time. First is to leave room in your allotted time to answer questions from the audience. The second method is to prepare a

written handout containing your main points and the facts associated with them. Always provide full contact information on any handouts so people can reach you in the future for further information.

When giving presentations with visual aids such as PowerPoint or some other slide-type program, your outline becomes the basis for the headlines and subheads shown on the screen. Choose key words and phrases that will trigger your memory of the points from the narrative that you want to make for each slide. Avoid putting long sentences on the slide. Your audience will read the sentences rather than listen to you. Full sentences also tempt you to read them out loud rather than speak naturally to your audience. Use just enough words to give the audience an expectation of what they are about to hear. If you have provided your presentation printed in outline form for note-taking, these words, along with notes taken, will help attendees remember your main points.

The narrative can be written in a separate document, or added into the notes section that does not show on the screen during the presentation. Again, avoid the temptation to read from the notes. Know the material well enough to be able to speak from the outline points that show on the screen.

Another form of oral presentation is a question-and-answer (Q&A) period. The length of time allowed is predetermined by an agenda. You may be offered some time to make some opening remarks, followed by answering questions from the audience. This extemporaneous method of oral presentation requires enough preparation that you have an encyclopedic knowledge of the material to be covered.

Your opening remarks are like the executive summary in a written report. You state the most important information you wish your audience to know. It could be your reasons for or against a planned change, or your explanation of how or why something happened. The educational process occurs in your answers to their questions and includes a written handout containing your main points and facts. You may also consider taking notes and later preparing a written follow-up that summarizes the information covered and answers questions in more detail than was possible during the session.

THE PRESS

Establishing a relationship with the press works best when you take a proactive approach. Reach out to your local media. Offer yourself as their first call for information about your agency. One way to do this is to prepare and distribute press releases on a regular basis. Once the local media get used to receiving material from you, they will expect and even look forward to it. Your information, presented properly, will help them reach their readership on a topic that is important to the public. Since they likely do not have the expertise to thoroughly cover emergency medical services, they will appreciate your assistance in helping their paper, radio station, or television channel cover an essential public service.

Go back to your list of media contacts and find out their preferred method for receiving press releases. Follow their instructions to the letter. The easier you can make it for them to use your material, the more likely it will appear in print.

Press releases follow a certain structure. Because news in newspapers is presented in the space remaining after the advertising is placed on the page, you can never be sure your entire press release will be used. To make sure the most important details get in, write your press release in the classic newspaper inverted pyramid style. This means the most important information is at the beginning of the release.

Best Practice

The City of Centralia (Washington) Fire Department inside the city, and Lewis County Fire District (FD) 12, which served unincorporated areas surrounding Centralia, provided fire and EMS services over a combined area of 180 square miles. Population and land use range from a dense urban core in Centralia to open land and forests in the rural fire district. With approximately 18,000 population to serve, the departments were collectively running approximately 3,500 calls per year, and by 2007 the number was increasing.

With call volume and population growth, Centralia and FD 12 had been running automatic mutual aid for fire and EMS calls. By 2007, the concurrent responses had made them, in an operations sense, one agency as both departments responded with each other on a daily basis. Leaders of both departments then crafted a plan to create a regional fire authority to make the two departments into one, operationally, financially, and administratively. Voters in both jurisdictions approved the plan in 2007. On January 1, 2008, the new merged agency began operations as Riverside Fire Authority (RFA).

EMS Levy Campaign

Fire service administrators crafted the fire authority ballot issue as a two-step process. Step one was the successful effort to win voter approval for the fire authority plan and create this new public taxing agency while formally ending the existing departments. In the fall of 2008, RFA went to the voters to approve step two: 50 cents per thousand dollars of assessed value, 10-year duration, property-tax EMS levy to generate the funding needed to expand advanced life support EMS services into the unincorporated areas formerly served by FD12.

Input for crafting the EMS levy message to the voters was essentially limited to in-house sources. Planning was centered around the assumption that the same voters who had approved the fire authority plan would naturally be inclined to vote to fund it as well. Besides, the public had already been forewarned that if the fire authority plan passed, the newly created agency would come back in 1 year for EMS funding.

Public messaging for passage of the EMS levy was limited to regionwide direct-mail campaigns and included these statements:

*   We told you this request would come now in the plan you authorized last year.
*   The revenue was needed to provide the level of ALS service the community was expecting.
*   Approve this funding for a 10-year term.

First Attempt: EMS Levy Failure

Washington state law requires property tax levies to pass with a minimum 60-percent positive vote. The EMS levy came in 31 votes short of that threshold. RFA leaders were surprised that the voters who "knew this was coming" rejected the levy measure. They immediately started talking with community members and examining the voting results to see what went wrong. It quickly became clear that RFA did not successfully communicate its message. Despite its efforts, voters were not clear what they were voting for and often voted based on incorrect information and assumptions.

Messaging Failures

*   Some assumptions were made.
*   It was somewhat taken for granted that voters would remember in the following year what they were asked to do the year before.
*   Voters in the city incorrectly assumed the EMS levy would be a double taxation on the property tax they already paid to the city.
*   Voters in the county incorrectly assumed they were already getting the service, so they thought "Why pay more?"
*   The double taxation fears led to a critical failure.
*   The 10-year duration also led to a critical failure.
*   The RFA had no history with county voters.
*   Voters struggled to understand how two fire departments had been dissolved and merged into one new entity, even though they had voted in favor of it just 1 year earlier. It was as if they believed there were now three departments.

Messaging Actions Taken

RFA leaders took several actions in response to this unsuccessful ballot measure, including the following:

*   Openly and publicly reducing staffing to only what could be paid for, which cut 24-hour staffing from two stations to one and the on-duty medic units from two to one. This drove home the message to voters that the funding status quo was inadequate to meet their needs.
*   Expanding the levy planning group to include more community involvement.

- Changing the messaging to make it more understandable by the recipient, not just internal audiences.
- Changing the message to explain how a yes vote would benefit the recipient, not RFA.

Critical fail factors convinced RFA leaders that their message had been poorly crafted from the standpoint of making voters understand why a positive vote was in their best interest. Their solution was to create a citizens' advisory committee to help craft a new message as the voice of the community. These individuals augmented the RFA members and leaders already on the committee to create a broad-based group that combined fire and EMS expertise with real-world feedback and suggestions.

Second-Effort Messaging to the Voters

Using input from the advisory committee, new messaging was created that emphasized answers to voters' "What's in it for me?" questions.

- Response delays from the very public closure of one station and stand-down of one medic unit were emphasized.
- The duration of the levy was reduced from 10 years to 6.

- A better explanation was crafted to show that it was not a double tax.
- A video was produced to add visual impact to the message. Key points were introduced, then reinforced by testimonial appearances by a local emergency department physician and from citizens who had been saved by EMS.

Passage

In the fall of 2009, voters approved the new EMS levy ballot measure. In January 2010, the second station and medic unit were reactivated. In looking back over the 2-year process, RFA Chief Jim Walkowski cites the three most critical messaging lessons learned:

1. Never assume anything, even in a climate where voters have historically been supportive.
2. You have to be able to explain technical and operational details to the voters in their own words, not industry jargon.
3. Your message has to be able to answer voters' "What's in it for me?" question before you will get any of their support or money.

As you continue to write, you add details in descending order of importance, ending with what is called a **boilerplate paragraph**. Boilerplate text contains a brief description of the agency and offers contacts for more information. Using the inverted style, editors can cut content from the bottom up to make the story fit the available space. As the cuts move from the bottom to the top, more and more details are lost. As long as the first paragraph remains, the essence of the message will get out.

The same holds true for press releases sent to radio and television stations. Instead of being limited by square inches on a page, stations are limited by how much airtime is avail-

able. Cutting from the bottom to fit a timed segment yields the same results as making the story fit on a page. As long as the first paragraph remains, you can make your point.

The all-important first paragraph of a news story is called the **lead**. In one or two sentences, the essential information of the story is presented by addressing the who, what, where, when, and why in relation to the topic.

Here's an example of a comprehensive, one-sentence lead:

"The Van Dyke Volunteer Ambulance Corps is holding a crab feed at its main station, 2812 Colonial Drive, on Saturday, June 16, to raise funds for its station remodel project."

Who: Van Dyke Volunteer Ambulance Corps

What: is holding a crab feed

Where: at its main station

When: Saturday, June 16

Why: to raise funds for its station remodel project

Press releases you send will mainly be associated with what is called **hard news**. This is information intended to inform and educate. Another useful type of story is called a **feature**. It is designed to entertain and go more into backgrounds, emotions, character studies, challenges faced and overcome, and personal triumphs. Where the hard news release is written in the inverted pyramid style, features are written in a circular style. The character(s) and situation are introduced, followed by the telling of the story, generally in chronological order. The feature closes the circle with a wrap-up that takes the reader back to information first introduced at the beginning.

Writing features is a more difficult and time-intensive process than drafting a simple press release. Unless you are an accomplished feature writer, you would better use your time contacting editors with a compelling story outline. The editor who chooses to do the story will assign it to a reporter who will do all the research and writing needed to bring your outline to life.

Another way to interact with the media is during a press conference. This can be a traumatic event for inexperienced or unprepared managers. Think of a press conference like any other Q&A session. Prepare as much as possible beforehand if the conference and topic have been scheduled in advance. If you suddenly find yourself in front of a microphone at a scene, answer truthfully from the knowledge and information you have available at the time. It is better to say "I don't have that information right now" than to make up something you may regret later. If possible, have someone you trust take notes so you can refer back

and get all promised information to the correct person. The notes are also a good teaching tool you can use to get better at doing off-the-cuff press conferences.

You should never mislead or misdirect reporters. If you really do not know, say so. If you know but are not at liberty to divulge the information, say so. When you say you do not have the information, that needs to be true. If you do have it but cannot release it, the press will think you have lied and you will lose their trust. The truth is always the best answer, even if it does not satisfy the questioner. Saying "Yes, I have that information but cannot release it at this time" keeps the information safe without compromising your relationship with the press.

WEB-BASED MESSAGES

Writing messages for the agency's website involves using both short and long forms of written communications. Use the short form when you do not have much time to capture someone's interest or answer questions. Web surfers stumbling onto your site need a striking visual or headline to capture their interest and make them click deeper into your site. Visitors coming to your site specifically to get some type of information need to be able to immediately and easily find a link to what they seek, or they will leave frustrated and unhappy with your agency.

Copy for landing pages—those pages that appear in response to clicking on links—needs to be short and descriptive, much like the lead paragraph of a news story. Say as much as you can on the page's topic in as few words as possible. Include words that you know or believe people may use as search terms in the copy. For example, on the page that talks about job requirements for paramedics, include words like *paramedic*, *jobs*, *hire*, *requirements*, *salary*, *training*, and your geographical location. Web visitors who put any of these terms into their web search tool are more likely to find your site near the top of the search results list, especially when location is used.

Inside or along with this brief landing page copy, include links to additional information located within the page or on other pages. This additional content can be unlimited in length and fully describe whatever topic is at hand, all without cluttering up the landing page. Remember to keep sentences brief. Long sentences are more difficult to read in the long lines of text across a computer screen.

In addition to your own website, use social media sites on the Internet to reach out, stay in touch, and inform people about your agency. There are hundreds of social media and social networking sites. To reduce that list to a number you can realistically maintain, check with your personnel, family, and friends to see which ones they frequent the most. Initially make a commercial page about your agency on the top three or four most popular sites they tell you. Because Internet social site popularity can change so quickly, follow trends to ensure your agency remains on the most popular ones.

When distributing press releases for a general audience, post them on your social media pages, too. Incident photos, noteworthy actions of personnel, accolades, new personnel information, upcoming classes or events—all can find a place on your website and your social networking pages. With them you can generate the information and make sure it gets posted without having to filter it through editors, as would be the case when sending material to the press.

Once established, publicize the social media pages, especially to personnel. Their participation, comments, and suggestions will help bring the pages to life and increase readership as their connections are exposed to the material.

■ USING DATA TO ADD CONTEXT ——

The outline of message categories offers a starting point when writing reports, presentations, press releases, and other materials for various audiences. Once the basic who, what, why, when, and where questions are answered, what is next? Certain data points can be used to add content, context, and fuller descriptions of the issue at hand. Although the data itself will change from one piece to the next, these data categories remain useful time after time.

Moving forward, let us say the new station that had been planned was built and has been in service for 2 years. During this period, much data that has been recorded and analyzed can be used to inform and educate audiences as needed.

FINANCIAL IMPACTS

The financial impacts of building and operating a new station for 2 years will be of great interest to stakeholders. Financial data can be used to satisfy a long list of questions budgetary and taxpayer stakeholders may pose to the agency.

Did the initial project finish at, under, or over budget? Why was the final cost different from projected costs in the budget? How do the ongoing costs compare to projections made prior to construction? If costs are higher, what is the reason and what adjustments have been made in the agency's operating budget to accommodate the additional ongoing expenses?

What sources of new revenue, if needed, have been found? On the other hand, if operating expenses have been less than anticipated, has the budget been reduced accordingly? If not, to what other area of the budget have the unused funds been shifted? Why were the funds shifted rather than the budget reduced?

Whether you are building a new station or just looking to change a single area of the budget, being able to answer these questions adds context to the columns of numbers and helps explain the processes followed to achieve the results being reported. Full disclosure results in a more informed audience.

THEN-VERSUS-NOW COMPARISONS

Some of the data that went into the original justifications for building the station can now be used as historical reference points. Benchmarks in many different areas become the "then" data for reporting "then-versus-now" comparisons. The comparisons may not always be positive, but nonetheless they must be reported in order to maintain credibility.

Choose data for the then-versus-now comparisons related to the new station based on the selling points offered to justify building the station. How have response times changed in the past 2 years with the new station in service? Has the call volume workload been spread more evenly among the stations as predicted? Have partners taken advantage of facilities and resources available as predicted? How has the public been able to use the station? Are there any unforeseen positive impacts to report from having the station, equipment, and personnel in service at that location?

Then-versus-now comparisons are valuable tools. In this case, a significant argument for building the new station was the positive impacts to be realized in many different areas. Two years later, how does the argument hold up? Find then-versus-now-comparisons in your own agency that can help you inform, educate, and drive discussions on your agency's future.

TRENDS

Compare the predictions made 2 years ago to the reality being documented every day and look for trends. Is call volume rising faster or slower than predicted? How have responders coped with working in the new station and all the operational changes that came along with it? Is use by partners and public groups increasing or decreasing?

Trends are a common benchmark for identifying problems or highlighting successes. Where individual occurrences may be just random chance, something that happens again and again can be examined to see if it is consistent enough to be called a trend. For example, calls to a local senior citizen community have increased over the past few months. Such increases usually are noticed first anecdotally by responders asking each other "Doesn't it seem like we're running more calls there than usual?"

A check of the run logs confirms 25 percent more calls in the last 6 months than has been the norm for that neighborhood. Looking at the individual reports, you see that the majority of the calls have been for falls. This trend data can now inspire public education efforts in that neighborhood for fall prevention.

PROJECTIONS

Making then-versus-now comparisons and following trends are the middle ground between past predictions and future projections. Comparisons prove how correct your original predictions were. Trends help you chart the course to the future as the basis for making new projections. Trends helped establish the need to build a new station 2 years ago. Using the same comparison and trending methods, projections can be made to determine when or if additional staffing and other resources will be needed, or even if an additional station will be required.

Data that go into making projections come from both outside and inside the agency. Outside influences can include trends in population growth or reductions, economic booms or busts, availability of primary health care for local residents, budgetary constraints from financial stakeholders, and scope of practice mandates from regulatory stakeholders. Internal trends show how external trends drive change within the agency in areas such as call volume, staffing needs, equipment acquisitions, budgets, and training requirements.

Using data to support projected decisions and requests shows a dedication to facts and the desire to excel in your job performance. Providing provable data also increases your credibility for any attempts at informing, educating, or persuading any of your audiences.

■ TELL THE STORY

Although hard data are important for making messages factual and bolstering arguments, a variety of ways are available to augment the facts and figures to clarify your point or to make the message more interesting. These storytelling techniques can be the central focus that the message is built around. On the other hand, they can be interjected into a message to break up dry sections of data-driven text and illustrate a point being made by that data.

ACTIONS TAKEN VERSUS ACTIONS CONSIDERED

When presenting the results of actions taken, including other options that were considered and not taken can be useful to help explain the thought processes that went into determining the final course of action. Oftentimes people reading or hearing about an activity will ask "Why didn't they do this instead?" Such questions can be posed in the form of criticisms from an uninformed person. Discussing other options considered, along with the reasons they were rejected and why the action used was correct, offers two benefits. First, this open dialogue can preempt questions that sound

critical. Second, it offers an opportunity to inform and educate the audience so they will better understand your agency's processes in the future.

In writing about the decision to build a new station, actions considered might have been increasing response capacity at existing stations or contracting the additional workload to an outside vendor. Follow up each action with an explanation of why the action taken was preferable.

TESTIMONIALS

Offering a **testimonial** from a satisfied customer is one of the oldest marketing tricks known. Interestingly enough, testimonials remain one of the most effective ways to encourage action, despite how much the technique is used. Agencies looking to persuade voters to approve a tax increase put former patients in their videos and advertising—with each patient's permission, of course. The patient looks robust and healthy, describes the terror at the time of the emergency, and credits the wonderful responders for saving them.

When looking for approval to build a new station, words from a resident of the area who supports the idea can be effective. Maybe the person supports the new station on its own merits, or perhaps the support stems from a family member who had a bad outcome because help was not closer. The individual goes on to say that the responders did everything they could, but too much time had passed, which was not their fault.

Personnel recruitment derives benefits from testimonials from current personnel appearing in ads and videos to say how much they like working for the agency. Public safety class announcements can feature a testimonial from a former participant who describes using CPR taught by the agency to save a loved one's life.

Testimonials work when the subject appears sincere and believable, speaks to the audience directly, and elicits an emotional response that meets the agency's goals.

HUMAN INTEREST STORIES

Human interest elements in published stories, or as the basis for a story, are popular because they give the reader a way to imagine themselves in that situation. Whether the reader thinks he or she can do the same thing, or is thankful for people who do what he or she never could, humanizing the story offers the writer an effective means of getting into the reader's head.

An example of inserting the human element would be in a report to stakeholders on the success of the citizen CPR classes being taught by the agency. The report would include all the data, such as number of classes held, number of people trained, and overall costs. Adding a human interest element about a CPR student later saving a loved one's life brings the message home that the classes have value. A reader could imagine being in the student's place and wonder if he or she could have performed as well, if at all.

The same report could be modified into a press release to illustrate to residents throughout the service area the value of learning CPR and, hopefully, to inspire more people to sign up for classes.

Coming at the same situation from a different angle, this human interest message could be a story about a citizen who saved her loved one. Written as a news feature, it would center around the citizen, how she decided to take the CPR class, how she reacted to the home emergency, how it has affected her, and what advice she has for others who do not know CPR. The agency moves from a starring to a supporting role in this type of story. However, the agency's goals of informing people about the agency's CPR classes and educating

them about the value of learning CPR remain intact.

QUOTES

Quotes are similar to testimonials in that people are used to help make a point. Where they differ the most is in length and who the quoted subject is. Where testimonials tell a story, quotes are more like sound bites. In a testimonial, someone who has been involved with the agency talks with admiration about the help received. The key element is the story itself.

The key elements of a quote are support for the position you are taking and the credibility of who said it. When looking to convince an audience to follow your recommendations, it can be helpful to get a supportive quote from someone with good name recognition and credentials. For capital fund-raising campaigns, nonprofit organizations have effectively used supportive quotes from politicians, business owners, celebrities, and others with high name recognition and good public images. Others who read the quotes are more likely to decide that if the person they admire is donating, then they will, too.

Quotes also attract donations from business owners who do not want a quoted competitor to look better or more generous.

As an example in an EMS agency, say you are drafting a message to financial stakeholders asking them to approve additional funds to purchase new equipment. Including a quote from your agency's medical program director stating that he agrees with this purchase can have great influence on their decision. The typical response is "If the doctor says the equipment is needed, it must be important."

PHOTOS

People respond to photos by placing themselves in the picture. (See Figure 6.3.) You see a photo of the Eiffel Tower in Paris, and you wish you were there. Parents see photos of

FIGURE 6.3 ■ People respond to photos by placing themselves in the picture.
Courtesy of Estero Fire Rescue.

kids having fun at a theme park and can imagine the delight on their own children's faces. Photos have the ability to transport the viewer to another time and place much more quickly and easily than words describing the same scene. For this reason, photos are a powerful informational and educational tool.

Use photos whenever and wherever possible to help explain the content of your message. A photo of the architect's rendering of the new station with a brief descriptive caption will give the reader more information much faster than an entire page of gray text. The viewer also will be much more likely to read and retain the accompanying text. When

selecting photos, use the same high standards as when you choose yours words. Poor photos of your agency at work can call your agency's overall level of professionalism into question.

Photos must be used carefully, though, to avoid any privacy or legal issues. As a general rule, photos of people or events in public on public property are fair to use. If the photos were shot at one of your agency's public events, it is never a bad idea to attempt to identify people and get their permission to use the photos in agency publications or on your website.

Photos also are a useful adjunct to testimonials and quotes. Citizens reading a testimonial and looking at a photo of someone who could be one of their neighbors help make your message hit home. When using a quote from a famous person, including a photo helps guarantee recognition from readers who might be unsure who the person is but will recognize the face, and vice versa.

VIDEO

With the advent of digital photography and video cameras even in cell phones, video has become as easy as still photography to capture and distribute. Video clips posted to the Internet can go viral and circulate around the world in mere hours. With video also comes sound, another distinct difference from still photography that can either help or hurt the agency.

As for still photos, quality is the key to credibility. Although professional-level work may not be necessary on video clips posted to your website and social media pages, simple cell-phone video will not reflect positively on the professionalism you wish to portray for your agency.

Like still photos, video testimonials can have a much greater impact than words. A grateful citizen appears on camera to describe an emergency. The video shows where the emergency happened—maybe in the home, or a crashed car in a junkyard. Emergency responders who worked the call are shown with your agency's name and apparatus prominently displayed. Describing this in detail with just words would take pages and require the reader to engage time and imagination to learn what happened. Telling the story with words and pictures would take several paragraphs, require less imagination, but still call for an investment of time to read and comprehend the message. A video clip can thoroughly tell the whole story in 90 seconds with virtually no effort on the viewer's part.

Videos are easily distributed, offer more information presented in less time, and only require minimal effort to comprehend. They can be a seriously effective informational and educational tool when used properly. However, as with photos, care must be taken to ensure that no images violate anyone's privacy or patient's rights. Agency guidelines should clearly state when or where photos or video may be used, by whom, under what circumstances, and what can and cannot be shown. Consult current legal opinions from EMS law experts for guidance.

CHAPTER REVIEW

Summary

Messages have no value if they use language the audience does not understand, do not answer the audience's questions, or are so lacking in style and substance that nobody spends enough time with them to get any information. The EMS manager who knows the agency's audiences and the kinds of questions they want answered is already prepared when an informational or educational need arises.

Just as the right information conveyed in the right language is important, the message must be crafted in a manner that takes advantage of whatever medium is used to send it. Understanding and taking advantage of the differences between written, spoken, and visual messages results in greater interest and comprehension from the audience.

Storytelling techniques are used to humanize dry details or persuade the audience to react in a desired way. The combination of data and emotion is an effective means of improving audience reaction to and retention of the information.

WHAT WOULD YOU DO? Reflection

Les used the five message categories he created to develop a Q&A-style outline for each audience. Under each category title, he listed the types of questions that audience would need answered. This outline became a checklist he could work from, modifying it to the topic at hand and ensuring the language he used covered all pertinent information that audience sought.

Les also drafted a second checklist of data points and storytelling techniques to select from while crafting messages. With the two checklists, he could be sure his messages were written in the right language for his audience, answer all anticipated questions, include all pertinent data, and contain other elements to help make the information more interesting and educational.

Review Questions

1. What is the difference between giving an ambulance demonstration to a group of elementary students and a group of paramedic students?
2. What is the purpose of an executive summary?
3. For what is a manual style used?
4. What type of style should you use when writing a press release? Why?
5. What is the first paragraph of a news story called?
6. What is the essential information in a story?
7. What is the difference between hard news and a feature?
8. What is the difference between making then-versus-now comparisons and trends?
9. For what are testimonials used?

Key Terms

boilerplate paragraph Description of and contact information about the entity sending the press release.

executive summary Brief discussion of the salient points and conclusions to be presented in detail in a report.

feature News story with an emphasis on the human-interest aspects of the topic being explored.

hard news Straightforward, fact-based description of a news event.

language Words, sentences, and paragraphs constructed to be understood by a targeted audience.

lead A clear, concise statement that introduces the facts of the story to its readers.

manual of style Reference document to follow for consistency in punctuation, capitalization, abbreviations, and other basic elements of writing.

reports Written accounts that formally document a particular matter.

sample outlines Writing tools that allow the author to add details in order to ensure the final document is thorough and targeted properly to its audience.

taxpayers Members of a community who provide funding from their own personal income for public services through payment of taxes.

testimonial Written or oral tribute.

Deliver the Message

Objectives

After reading this chapter, the student should be able to:

7.1   Describe how to use different written, oral, and electronic methods to effectively deliver information to audiences.

7.2   Discuss how to give effective oral presentations.

7.3   Explain how to maintain relationships with print and electronic media.

7.4   Describe how to use electronic media and social networking to inform and educate audiences.

Overview

This title identifies and offers examples of the informational and educational components that work together to form a comprehensive public relations plan. Capitalizing on successful strategies used in marketing and advertising, it explains the reasons why public information and education are necessary for gaining and holding the public trust.

Key Terms

blog	**really simple syndication (RSS)**	**sunshine meetings**

WHAT WOULD YOU DO?

You should try to catalog and learn to use all the different means for delivering messages in a manner to best ensure each is received by its target audience.

Courtesy of Ed Mund.

Despite all the work Les has put into defining his audiences and messages, he knows that carefully crafting a message in the right language is wasted effort if the message does not reach its intended target. Much like starting a trip to another town without knowing which road to take, the venture is doomed from the start. What Les needs to do is catalog and learn to use all the different means at his disposal for delivering messages in a manner to best ensure each is received by its target audience.

Questions

1. How can Les create a comprehensive catalog of message delivery methods?
2. How can he learn to use the different written, oral, and electronic methods effectively?

■ INTRODUCTION

We have an overwhelming number of choices for disseminating information, which offers us multiple opportunities to be successful. On the other hand, choosing which means to use from the multitudes available can be daunting. The EMS manager can overcome the challenge of making the right choice every time by studying what is available and most used among his targeted audiences. Just as advertisers choose to place their commercials where they can reach the largest number of desired viewers or listeners, the EMS manager should identify which delivery method will best serve the agency's needs depending on the message to be delivered and the intended audience.

Depending on the circumstance, the delivery method may be in person, in a report, via radio or television, or by some other electronic means. No matter which method is used, the common denominator for the EMS manager is thorough preparation and mastery of all facts prior to engaging the audience. Even oral presentations require research and some writing, even if the writing is only notes used to jog the memory when needed.

■ ORAL PRESENTATIONS

Most people are perfectly comfortable having a conversation on a familiar subject with another individual or even a small group in a casual setting. Yet they shrink from the chance to make an oral presentation to a group on the very same subject. The fear and sense of aloneness in front of a group are hard to shake, even when you know everyone in the audience.

Preparation and practice are the two routes to successful oral presentations.

OPPORTUNITIES

Start preparing to deliver messages by seeking opportunities to speak to your different targeted audiences. Research how each audience seeks and selects its speakers. Contact each audience to discuss possible presentation topics and schedule your appearance. Then craft messages that best serve your intent to inform, educate, or persuade the audience about the selected topic.

Stakeholders

Whether regulatory or financial in nature, stakeholder bodies hold meetings in order to conduct their business. In-person presentations in an open meeting offer great opportunities to present your information and ensure comprehension much more effectively than is possible with written reports. (See Figure 7.1.) In areas where governmental bodies are required to hold open, public **sunshine meetings** in order to consider actions, these meetings may be your only means of having your message heard.

You should be attending as many of these meetings as possible for at least three good reasons. First, it will give you an opportunity to observe how the meetings flow and how the stakeholders interact with others in the room. Second, showing enough interest to attend meetings even when you are not on the agenda will leave a positive image of you in the stakeholders' minds.

Finally, observing how others make presentations to the stakeholders, and how they interact during the presentation, will give you valuable clues on how to best prepare your own presentations. How long should it be? Is

FIGURE 7.1 ■ In-person presentations in an open meeting offer great opportunities to present your information and ensure comprehension much more effectively than is possible with written reports.
Source: © *auremar/Fotolia*

a transcript of your comments desired, or just an outline? Do all points made in the presentation also need to be proved on the spot, or can you present the salient points and provide printed background materials? Note what kind of questions you can anticipate being asked, and have information ready and prepared handouts to respond to them.

Partners

Partners work together best when they know one another, both personally and professionally. Seek opportunities to engage partners in sharing information. Reports and email exchanges have great merit when it comes to setting up meetings or capturing volumes of information. Nevertheless, there is no substitute for person-to-person connections when it comes to understanding each other's needs and intentions. Questions can be asked and answered on all sides. Everyone leaves the interaction with the same information and a better understanding of the information that was presented.

One way partners can work together in person is to contact the partner or partners with whom you want to share information and arrange meetings. Just as you would do when presenting to stakeholders, have printed materials for the partners to take back with them to their own agencies or companies.

Another way for partners to work together is to create an information-sharing group with representatives from all common partners as members. Establish a routine meeting schedule with an agenda that gives all partners an opportunity to keep everyone else informed of activities, policies, capabilities, and procedures that affect interaction between each organization and its partners. Use this meeting to seek input and advice from your partners when you are considering an issue that will affect them as well as your own agency. Their input in the early stages will help ensure their buy-in when your issue begins to require their participation.

The Public

Opportunities to speak to the public are limited only by the number of groups in your area and the amount of time you or your designees have to devote to this valuable activity. Schools, neighborhood associations, political groups, service clubs, and special-interest societies all have something in common with the services your agency provides. Reach out to these groups to seek that common ground, then prepare presentations that both interest them and promote your informational and educational goals.

Community service clubs with weekly meetings are especially eager for speakers. (See Figure 7.2.) To meet this weekly demand, many appoint a member to ensure each meeting features a speaker of interest to the group. Become acquainted with such members in your community's service clubs. Learn what interests your agency and the club share, or what public service projects you can partner on. Provide every point person with a list of presentations and speakers from your agency that will help them fill their speaker's calendars and allow you to inform and educate their members on a variety of important topics. You or someone from your agency may also choose to join a service club to help the club do its community work and be a constant reminder and resource about the agency.

Public speaking can present prime recruiting opportunities. Recruiting can be the overall theme of the presentation, especially to high school and college students looking to select careers. However, recruiting can also be a part of every presentation, in particular for agencies that rely on volunteers to fill certain roles. As you talk about a service the agency provides, detail how volunteers help the agency do its job, from clerical help to direct patient care.

Figure 7.2 ▪ Community service clubs with weekly meetings are especially eager for speakers. *Courtesy of Ed Mund.*

Expand your outreach by participating in public events such as health fairs and health promotion events. Set up and staff a booth at county fairs, farmers' markets and community celebrations.

Develop a packet that includes an application, descriptions of paid and volunteer positions, minimum requirements to volunteer or be hired, an outline of initial and ongoing training requirements, and a calendar of hours the volunteer applicant can expect to devote in the first 12 months. When speaking before different groups, carry a supply of these packets with you and be ready to hand them out on request.

Press Conferences

Press conferences are a useful means of reaching many media outlets at one time. (See Figure 7.3.) In a single meeting, you can deliver your message that would otherwise take hours or days were you doing one interview at a time.

Press conferences should not be taken lightly, though. Reserve them for important events of great newsworthiness, not routine business. It costs more in time and money for reporters to attend a press conference than to conduct a telephone interview from their desk. Make your press conference worth their while, or you will quickly wear out your welcome.

Examples of press conference-worthy topics include major new equipment that dramatically expands the agency's capabilities, significant awards or recognition, new personnel at top levels, a major event or milestone in the agency's history, and a current major event in which agency played a key role that is likely to be widely remembered in the history of the community.

Arrange for a scribe at the press conference to list everyone in attendance and to take notes. By the end of the day, if possible, produce a transcript or at least a detailed outline of what was covered and send it to all media outlets in

FIGURE 7.3 ■ Press conferences are a useful means of reaching many media outlets all at one time. *Courtesy of Estero Fire Rescue.*

attendance. Engage a photographer if the press conference involves more than just one or two people talking. Get photos of the equipment, the key people who participate in the press conference, the people who are recognized or introduced, and the disaster scene if relevant.

Do not penalize media outlets that are not in attendance. You may not know why they did not or could not send a reporter, so do not assume it was because of a snub or any malicious intent on their part. Treat everyone the same, even when you do know that the media outlet is not supportive of the agency. Send those not in attendance the same scribe's report and photos from the conference that you provide to attendees.

Talk Show Interview

If your area's radio and television stations have local celebrity talk shows, these can be good opportunities to spread important mes-

sages. Each program has a number of interview slots to fill for every broadcast. Booking staff for these shows are eager to consider offers from local public service agencies. Much like having people with high levels of name recognition publicly support your agency's efforts, a local media celebrity's positive treatment of you and your agency during a program will encourage their viewers to think highly of your agency.

Watch or listen to several broadcasts before you are on air to get a feel for the host, audience, and callers if applicable. Have a central theme or messaging goal of the conversation arranged with the host, and be prepared with enough information to more than fill the amount of time allotted. Be familiar with how the host asks questions. Are guests allowed to show their knowledge? Does the host talk the most, leaving little time for replies? Is the host combative or friendly, disruptive or respectful? How does the audience participate? Does the host interview for the camera, or perform for the audience at the guest's expense? Are you allowed to bring props or visuals on television shows?

When participating on live radio talk shows, it is preferable to arrange an in-studio interview over a phone-in chat. The audio quality will be better for the listeners. You will benefit from being able to see the host's body language and expressions during the interview. Your presence will command more of the host's attention as he or she observes your body language and expressions. Again, have a central theme or message goal arranged with the host, and listen to the program ahead of time to help prepare yourself for your best performance.

Remember, in radio interviews the audience cannot see you, so you must illustrate important concepts and emphasize important points through voice inflection and vocal descriptors. It pays to be energized and somewhat animated during radio interviews so that the audience can "hear" your gestures.

Local Cable TV

Local cable television operators offer a public access channel for community groups and individuals to broadcast local-origin programs. Search the listings and watch local-access channel programs in your area to see if one or more is a fit for your agency. Develop content to elicit an invitation, then prepare just like for any other television host interview. Prepare a topic, study the program and how the host works, and schedule the time to be a guest.

Shift Briefing

In addition to the training elements discussed at shift briefings, these gatherings are a great opportunity to get personnel into the public information and education loop. (See Figure 7.4.)

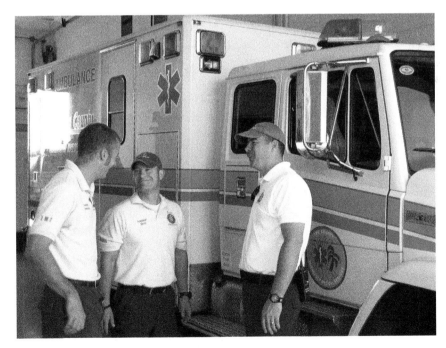

FIGURE 7.4 ▨ In addition to the training elements discussed at shift briefings, these gatherings are a great opportunity to get personnel into the public information and education loop. *Courtesy of Jeffrey T. Lindsey, Ph.D.*

In just a few minutes, you can cover topics that will give them the knowledge and tools to help the agency reach its messaging goals. Every time agency personnel interact with the public, whether in the station, on a call, at the grocery store, or elsewhere, they have an opportunity to inform, educate, and even recruit.

Topics for shift briefings can include department news the public can or should hear, special recognitions, correcting messaging errors, tips for talking to the public on calls or during downtime, and recruiting for upcoming opportunities to assist public outreach efforts. Be sure to offer training, tutoring, or coaching to improve the quality of interaction with the public. The more people in the agency spreading quality information, the better the public will be educated on matters important to the agency.

SPEAKING TIPS

Arranging speaking opportunities is the first half of getting your message across to a desired audience. The second half is the ability to be an effective speaker. Devote as much time, energy, and practice to developing presentation skills as you would to honing any other important skills. Scores of self-help books and other sources for information are available. One short, but comprehensive, book is the *New York Times* and *Wall Street Journal* bestseller *The Exceptional Presenter* by Timothy Koegel (2007).

Become an Exceptional Presenter

Koegel uses the acronym OPEN UP to describe the six characteristics of an exceptional presenter. The letters stand for:

- Organized
- Passionate
- Engaging
- Natural
- Understand Your Audience
- Practice (Koegel, 2007, p. 4)

Developing and incorporating each of those six characteristics into a presentation will allow the exceptional speaker to own the room. This means the speaker has mastered the art of public speaking to the point where the audience is captivated and responds in total confidence that what the speaker is saying is true and worthy of their time.

Presentation Components

One key to a successful presentation is simply showing up early. If possible, arrive up to 60 minutes before your scheduled speaking time. Use the time to check out the room's size, layout, and acoustics. (See Figure 7.5.) Engage in conversation with people as they arrive for the presentation to get a sense of who they are and what they are expecting of you.

If possible, have your equipment up and running no less than 20 minutes prior to the starting time. This will give you and local technicians time to iron out any equipment compatibility issues or malfunctions. Have backup plans in place for equipment and the presentation itself. When using a computer-based presentation, try to use the computer with which you are most familiar. In addition, carry a self-contained copy of the presentation on CD and portable disc drive in case mechanical failure or system incompatibility renders your computer useless. With either the CD or portable drive, you should be able to install and run your presentation on the host's system.

Your backup plan should also account for the possibility of not being able to use your computer-based presentation. Have a printed copy of the presentation you can refer to while speaking. Use drawing boards in the room or flip charts to sketch key visuals from the presentation, such as charts or graphs that are essential to delivering your message. If you have been able to distribute notes to the audience prior to your presentation, they will have your original visuals to refer to, even if only in miniature or black and white.

FIGURE 7.5 ■ Arrive up to 60 minutes before your scheduled speaking time. Use the time to check out the room's size, layout, and acoustics. *Courtesy of Jeffrey T. Lindsey, Ph.D.*

Once you begin the presentation, you want to tell your audience three times what the contents are. This is commonly described as "Tell them what you are going to tell them, tell them, and then tell them what you just told them." Begin with an outline of your presentation's objectives: "Here is what we will talk about today." The body of the presentation fills in the details that accomplish the objectives. Your conclusion recaps the objectives and how they were met.

End each presentation with a purpose statement telling the audience what you want or expect of them after you speak. It may be a call to action to become engaged in an issue or process. It may be a caution to be aware of the concerns just presented. Whatever your purpose is, craft the statement around what you want the audience to remember if they only remember one thing from your presentation.

Research Your Audience

Researching your audience is an essential part of preparing your presentation. Your message must be crafted in language most likely to meet your goals to inform, educate, and, where applicable, persuade audience members. First, ascertain the purpose of group. What, if any, community service or function does the group fulfill? Why does the group meet, and what do members seek to get out of membership and attendance?

Who belongs to the group? Answer this question generally by finding what common denominator binds these individuals together. Also answer it individually, taking note of what prominent or influential local citizens are members or leaders of the group.

Best Practice

Riverside Fire Authority (RFA) is a fire-based Advanced Life Support EMS agency serving 180 square miles in and around the city of Centralia, Washington. In September 2008, RFA placed an EMS levy property tax measure on the ballot asking taxpayers in its service area to pay 50 cents per thousand dollars of assessed value to pay for ALS-level services throughout RFA's response area. Washington state law requires property tax increase requests to pass with a minimum 60-percent positive vote. This request came in 31 votes short of the 60-percent threshold.

Delivering the Message: First Levy Attempt Failed

Failure to pass the EMS levy on the first attempt was shown to be caused by a combination of poor messaging and insufficient outreach. Ways to improve the message were studied and implemented by RFA. However, the right message is still useless if the voters don't hear it. The only message delivery used on the first levy attempt was regionwide direct-mail campaigns. RFA leaders concluded that equally important to having the right message was significantly expanding efforts to deliver the message to all voters.

Second Try to Reach the Voters

RFA leaders used a community advisory committee to help develop more ways of delivering the message to the voters.

- All advertising and promotional materials contained references to a newly produced video, which recorded more than 4,000 hits on YouTube and the RFA websites.
- Newspaper and billboard advertising paid for by the firefighters' union local appeared with voter-friendly language.

- A local talk radio program host was an outspoken opponent of the EMS levy. Airtime was purchased to run ads favoring the levy during his show.
- The local daily newspaper granted space for guest columns written by the RFA chief, and printed numerous letters to the editor from RFA personnel and local community leaders.
- Community leaders helped connect RFA leaders with community groups and neighborhood associations to make in-person presentations. The video was shown, questions answered, and leave-behind materials distributed.
- A new direct-mail campaign with better messaging and more frequent mailings was done.
- When appropriate, responders used contacts made while running calls as opportunities to explain the measure to citizens.

Passage

In the fall of 2009, voters approved the second EMS levy ballot measure. In January 2010, a second fire station was staffed and its medic unit activated. In looking back over the 2-year process, RFA Chief Jim Walkowski cites the three most critical message-delivery lessons learned:

1. You have to use every means available to reach enough voters to earn passage.
2. Getting community members involved to help craft the message in their own words and direct how it was spread was the single most effective factor in the second levy's passage.
3. Let others outside the agency step up and help carry your message to their own circle of influence.

Know why the group invited you to speak. If the group invited you, ask what the group wants to hear or learn from your presentation. Then ask again at the beginning of your presentation. At the point where you are outlining your objectives, invite the audience to speak to their own curiosities.

Presentation Style

Everyone has their own style of speaking. What makes exceptional speakers different is their ability to augment their natural talents with learned behaviors in order to be comfortable delivering organized, well-practiced presentations with an obvious passion. Audiences hear your words, but assimilate more of your message through your posture, body language, and voice. If you do not appear engaged in the presentation, your audience will not be either.

Preparation and practice will keep you looking relaxed as if you know the subject inside and out—because you do. Use visual aids to enhance, not distract from, what you are saying. Unless you want the audience to follow along on a handout as you speak, handouts other than brief notes should be distributed after you speak. Giving the audience something to focus on other than what you are saying will diminish their attention and reduce their retention of your presentation.

Few people are comfortable speaking in front of a group of people, so controlling fear is another essential step toward becoming an exceptional presenter. Knowing your presentation thoroughly will help you overcome the fear of missing something. At the same time, it is not the end of the world if you forget to include a random detail or less-than-critical illustrative point. Do not try to tell the audience everything you know, just what is in the presentation that covers your objectives. Rehearse again and again and again, out loud, until the presentation becomes as effortless

as having a conversation on the phone with a trusted friend.

Engage Your Audience

You have already begun interacting with the audience by arriving early. Be sure to build time into your presentation to allow interaction with the audience. Depending on the environment, there may be opportunities to engage the audience during or after the presentation or both. If the room permits, square up to the person who is addressing you, make eye contact, show that person you are listening and valuing his input.

Use stories, examples, and anecdotes to help describe or explain a concept in language the audience will understand. Smile. If you know someone's name, use it when addressing them. Read your audience to know when they are listening intently or when you have lost them over some technical matter it appears they do not understand. On longer presentations, watch for clues that your audience needs a break, even if this does not happen at the time you had a break planned.

Honor all input from the audience, even if you do not agree with what the person is saying. Do not belittle or demean any statements. If you disagree, politely present your own evidence without dismissing the person's belief or evidence.

Handling Questions

As you engage the audience, people will want to ask questions. Sometimes due to the environment, this can only be done at the end of the presentation or afterward. In smaller groups with less stringent time constraints, questions can be asked and answered during the presentation. This is a sure way to get audience members involved and for you to learn whether or not your message is being understood. If you have rehearsed enough, interruptions for questions will not throw you off when it is time to return to your prepared remarks.

Remember, there is no such thing as a stupid question from the audience. Never belittle an audience member through impatience, facial expressions, rolled eyes, heavy sighs, words, or posturing, no matter how inconsequential you think a question asked may be. Any projection of superiority or boredom on your part will remove any goodwill you have gained with the audience, probably permanently. On the other hand, actively acknowledging and engaging with the questioner will improve your rapport with the entire audience. Your answers need to always be factual and, if possible, referenced. Add credibility to your information by providing its source.

Your audience will most remember the last thing you say. At the end of a post-presentation question-and-answer session always remember to smile, thank the audience, and repeat the purpose statement so it is the last thing they hear.

■ WRITTEN PRESENTATIONS ———

There are many opportunities to inform and educate via the written word. One of the best advantages of that is the ability to use the same written piece over and over in multiple ways. Unlike oral presentations that only reach exceptional numbers through much repeated effort, one written piece, such as a press release, can multiply its reach many times over with no appreciable additional work on your part.

MAINTAIN RELATIONSHIPS WITH LOCAL PRINT MEDIA

Maintain a current contact lists that includes who is who at your local print media. Learn these names by reading newspapers as thoroughly as possible and by periodically reaching out to your main contact at each one. In small communities with weekly and biweekly newspapers, your main contact may be one person with many titles: publisher, editor, reporter, photographer, and ad salesperson. Elsewhere, the staff may be larger, but you should still be aware of each person's defined duties and responsibilities.

Editors

Editors are the gatekeepers of the news coming into the newspaper office and going into the paper. Editors set the rules for contact and submission to their papers. They may assign a news reporter as your primary contact, or prefer you always go through them with your press release submissions or story queries. When editors change, be sure to quickly introduce yourself to the new editor and ascertain the contact methods the new editor wants you to follow.

If the editor gives you a free hand to work with news reporters, columnists, feature writers, and photographers directly, establish contact with them and file away information on how they prefer to be reached, especially outside of regular business hours.

The editor is also your first reference point for press release technical specifications. Pay close attention to the writing style, page formatting, and means of submitting the piece that the paper specifies. Any requirement you do not follow reduces or possibly eliminates chances of that press release being considered, especially in a busy or understaffed newsroom. The closer you can make your press release to being exactly as it will appear in print, the less work the editor has to do, and the better its chances of being published.

Finally, and most important, deadlines matter. There is an old saying in the news business that "Nothing is deader than dead news." If you do not submit your press release before the deadline, do not be surprised if it is not printed. If you routinely fail to meet deadlines, you will lose professional credibility with the editor and may never get anything published.

Reporters and Columnists

When working with newspaper writing staff, it is important to know what different types of stories the different writers produce. News reporters focus on what is known as hard news. Their stories tell who, what, where, when, and why related to a particular event. Their focus with you will be on answering those questions and getting as many pertinent facts as possible into the story. They are not interested in whether the story is good or bad for the agency—only that the facts are reported as they understand them.

To use a sports analogy, news reporters are the play-by-play announcers. Features reporters are the color commentators. The latter write from a human-interest point of view, though they include facts, but they also include background and descriptions that add interest and humanity to the story. As an example, let us say your agency has just publicly unveiled its original ambulance, fully restored to its brand-new glory. A hard news reporter would give specifications on the ambulance, who led and participated in the restoration effort, how many hours and dollars went into the project, and what future uses the agency will have for the ambulance. The features reporter's story will include how the restoration effort was inspired, offer memories from the one remaining retired agency responder who used to drive the ambulance, describe the community effort that helped acquire the vehicle, and relate some of the famous events in which the ambulance played a role.

Some newspapers also have local single-topic columnists who write on a regular basis. Generally, these writers have an umbrella theme that ties together all their columns.

Learn their themes, and read back issues to see how they approach the topics and write their columns. Find out if you may contact them directly or must work through the editor. Then seek opportunities to tie an informational need to their themes.

As an example, a retired editor or schoolteacher may do a weekly column on how life used to be in the community 50 years or more ago. Contact them with historical information about an important anniversary coming up for the agency. Then-and-now stories will be of great interest to these columnists.

If the paper has a current events columnist, keep that writer supplied with press releases and short tidbits of information about upcoming events, new services, classes offered, and milestones reached.

Community newspapers often engage columnists from outlying rural areas to submit news from their communities. If your agency serves or has stations in these rural areas, feed the community columnist information about calls, new personnel, seasonal safety reminders, announcements of classes and public events, and anything else new at the station.

Photographers

Establish a rapport with your area newspapers' photographers. Learn what content, visuals, and accessibility they are looking for at emergency scenes and find ways to help meet their needs. See if you can get access to their photographs and use them for your agency's website or other purposes, with full attribution for the photographer and paper.

Determine whose permission you need to call the photographer directly with tips from a scene at any hour or from your office. Find out if the paper is willing to accept outside photos from your agency. If so, learn and follow the paper's technical specifications for submitting photos. File the specs by media outlet and check back periodically to see if technology or equipment changes have altered their specifications.

WRITING REPORTS

Whether you are writing to educate, document, or persuade, the language used in a report will be dependent on the audience targeted. Present facts without bias or opinion, even when writing to persuade. Do not tell the reader how to think. Unsubstantiated opinions from a writer who the reader may have no reason to implicitly trust or agree with will prove fruitless. Instead, lead the reader to reach the conclusion you desire through use of verifiable data logically presented in a manner that precludes any other reasonable judgment.

Inform your readers in an executive summary, and then educate them in the body of the report with all the data behind the summary. This is being courteous of your readers' time and increases the odds of your report being read. Another courtesy is to include a table of contents. If a particular item in the summary piques someone's interest, a robust table of contents will direct the reader to where he or she can more fully learn about the topic without having to read the entire report, unless so desired.

From our earliest days in school, we ask about any new writing assignment "How long does it have to be?" The correct answer in this case is that it only has to be long enough to cover the subject. Again, be courteous of your readers' time. When in doubt, shorten it. However, be aware that you can remove too much. Because of your knowledge of the information being written, it is possible for your brain to fill in details that are no longer on the page. Another reader will not do this. After removing information to shorten a section, use an independent reviewer unfamiliar with the content to test whether or not enough information remains to cover the subject.

Use photos and illustrations to help explain content and break up pages of gray text. A single photo of the inside of an ambulance compartment along with the piece of new equipment that obviously cannot fit inside instantly does the same job as lots of words mixed with measurements. For anyone, it tells the story faster. For visual learners, it tells the story better than words can. Be sure to always include a caption describing, or at least labeling, what is in the photo and identifying every person.

When preparing an important report for distribution, be aware that there is a fine line between looking serious versus looking like too much time and money were spent on the report. A good rule of thumb is to see what other similar reports prepared for the same audience look like, and to find out how they were perceived by the audience. You want your report to have a look that represents how much effort went into it and how seriously it should be taken. However, too much color, flashy graphics, and fancy bindings can work against you, especially if the report includes requests for funding.

Do not assume that the report will necessarily be printed. If permitted by the audience, consider electronic distribution via CD, email, intranet, or Internet. When formatting the report for electronic distribution, do not assume that every potential reader will use the same computer hardware and software that you do to view it. Test CDs in different but common computer brands and operating systems, ranging from those that are current to those that are several years old. View emailed versions using different brands of email software and preference settings. View Internet versions using different browsers and operating systems. Make any necessary adjustments to the report's formatting and file type to ensure that no reader is unable to access the information.

CREATING BROCHURES AND PAMPHLETS

In today's electronic world, there is still a place for printed informational and educational materials. Paper materials are cheap to produce in quantity and easy to distribute. Paper is easy to carry in quantity on rigs, stack on tables, and stuff in brochure racks. It folds into a pocket for easy transportation. Paper products can be saved and referred to again and again.

Brochures and pamphlets are generally differentiated by size and complexity. A pamphlet, also sometimes called a leaflet, is usually a single sheet of paper with information on one or both sides. Often it is not folded and presents its information in one visual sweep, left to right, top to bottom. Brochures are more complicated, with folds, multiple panels, possibly multiple pages, and a visual design that leads the reader from one panel to another, one page to the next. The amount of information you need to include is the primary reason behind choosing one form over the other.

The fact sheets on your website are a great start for building a catalog of necessary printed materials. You have, in effect, ready-made pamphlets. They can be printed on demand one at a time, or in quantity for public events as the need arises. Because they are only printed as needed, they can be easily updated immediately prior to printing so only the latest, most accurate information is ever distributed.

Prioritize what to have printed according to your need to widely disseminate the information. Public safety information and ongoing programs are frequent topics of interest to the public.

Brochures can be created and provided for responders to hand out at the right time on appropriate calls. Topics could include cardiac and stroke symptoms, fall prevention, a bicycle helmet program, injury prevention for different ages, and carbon monoxide warnings.

Work with partners to share content and costs. State health and safety agencies may have information and even preprinted materials you can use at little or no cost. Companies with a vested interest in health and safety— auto and medical insurance companies, for example—offer information and produce materials for distribution at marginal or no cost.

Brochures and pamphlets provide little space for content, so think carefully about what to include. Realize that there may not be enough room to do more than inform and offer contacts for additional details. Because of the desire to say as much as possible in a limited space, wise use of quality photos to illustrate and educate is necessary.

Determining how many copies to print is a question that confounds many people. They know what they want the brochure to say, and have opinions on how it should look, but have no idea how to estimate how many to print. A good rule of thumb on print quantity is to consider how long you expect the information in the brochure to remain valid and the anticipated number to be distributed during that time frame. Use historical references when possible. For instance, if you typically use 500 bike helmet brochures each year at a community safety fair and the brochure copy remains valid for 2 years, order 1,000 brochures at the next printing.

Budget for professional help when developing brochures and pamphlets. The final printed product will be a reflection of the agency. You want that reflection to project the same professionalism and quality that you show on your uniforms, ambulances, and stations. The airline industry knows that passengers who see torn upholstery worry about the condition of the entire airplane. You do not want someone looking at a poorly produced brochure and in response worrying about the quality of your patient care. If your own budget is not sufficient, seek help from partners and include information they provide in your brochure. If your budget is still too low, consider using graphics or art class students from a local college or trade school.

Although it is true that many software packages can help you design a brochure, the software will only produce what the user directs it to do. The user has to know graphic design principles and methods, then use the software to turn ideas into a layout to be printed. Just as handing someone a hammer does not turn them into an expert carpenter, buying software will not create a qualified graphic designer.

COMMUNITY NEWSLETTER

Many agencies find it useful to budget for production of a community newsletter on a recurring basis. This gives the agency an effective means to place messages into homes and businesses throughout its response area. With current technology, it is simple to produce a printed newsletter for direct mail, along with an identical version for distribution electronically and posting on the agency's website.

Content can include safety messages tied to the time of year the newsletter issue is being published, upcoming public events, classes offered, news about the agency, new equipment, new personnel, awards and recognitions, recruiting solicitation, and a personal message from the chief. The newsletter also offers an opportunity for the agency to address a community need or concern from its own perspective in a way not afforded by the local press.

Newsletters should be published often enough for people to find them useful, but not so often that people question the amount of money being spent in a way some would consider negatively as wasteful or self-promoting. Quarterly throughout the year is a commonly used, safe interval. The 3-month interval also allows the editor to develop content in spite of an otherwise busy work schedule.

Several factors are weighed when constructing a newsletter budget. First, budget for professional design assistance. Hire professionals to create the newsletter's design standards and flag—the title and accompanying artwork and information at the top of page one. Other design standards include page size, number of columns, font type and size for headlines, body text, and picture captions. You may have the designer also produce each issue to print-ready status, or provide you with a template that you can use to lay out each issue, depending on your level of expertise.

Another budget factor is printing. This expense is determined by the size of the page, number of pages, ink color(s), weight and brand of paper used, and type of folding and bindery processes. Finally, factor in distribution costs, whether done internally, by a courier service, or via direct mail. If using direct mail, you will need to have a postal permit and use U.S. Postal Service instructions to sort and package newsletters into bundles your local postmaster will accept for direct mailing. After doing all the sorting and bundling work, you then take the newsletters to the same post office that issued your mailing permit and prepay the postage fee based on the number of newsletters you deliver to be mailed.

If your direct-mail newsletter goes to more than 1,000 addresses, you should consider hiring a mailing service to do the bundling, packaging, and delivery for you. Some printers may also offer a mailing service, or will recommend one they prefer using. One fee generally covers handling costs and the use of a mailing permit the printer owns. You will still have to pay postage at the time the newsletters are delivered to the post office.

■ AUDIO PRESENTATIONS ─────

Writing for audio presentations is similar to writing a speech. You may be constrained by the overall length of time permitted. While writing, read sentences aloud to see how words flow one into another. Avoid harsh sounds, like multiple consonants in succession: *The crashing of kicked cans caromed off the cars and echoed for blocks.* Avoid tongue twisters where multiple letter combinations doom the speaker to fail: *She sells sea shells by the sea shore.* Also be aware of how sentences sound flowing into one another.

Write in less than one-breath sentences. You can also break up longer sentences into one-breath sections. For example: *When we last saw the ambulance crew—Larry, Kris, and Mandy—they were running down the hillside toward the car at the bottom of the ravine.*

MAINTAIN RELATIONSHIPS WITH RADIO STATIONS

If you have radio stations serving your community, maintain relationships with the stations' assignment editors and producers. They determine who your station contacts are for news and announcement submissions. Use your assigned contact person to establish how to reach other staff members, especially on-air personalities. Listen to their on-air personalities to learn their styles, what kind of local news and events they like to talk about, and what common ground your agency can offer to encourage working together. Appear on talk radio programs when you have a specific message to send, and interact with callers' questions to help educate the audience.

RADIO NEWS

News does not stop. Electronic news on radio, television, and the Internet have an instantaneous appetite for material. Make yourself or a designee available to comment any time, around the clock, whenever news happens. It may not even be related to your agency. It may be an event featuring a partner agency or stakeholder about which someone in your position may have background information to share.

Keep a file of how each news station prefers to receive press releases. Send them the same releases you send to other media outlets and let them edit for the length they want. Pay close attention to the lead, remembering that you have to paint a visual picture with words. Radio offers no opportunity for photographic or video augmentation. You may get 10 inches of news in the local paper, but the same story may be condensed into just 10 seconds of airtime for your lead.

In addition to routine press releases, try to get major event news to the station before it calls you. Preempt bad questions from uninformed reporters by providing facts, figures, and details that will either satisfy their curiosity or lead them to ask questions that are more thoughtful.

UPCOMING EVENTS

In addition to feeding information to the station's newsroom, stay in touch with its contest and sales staff. Watch for any opportunity to participate in or even co-sponsor community events the radio station plans or features. Learn what you need to do to have a radio station do live remotes at your own public events. If more than one radio station in your area does live remotes at community events, make arrangements to share your opportunities among them.

PROVIDING AUDIO FILES

Radio stations all have their own standards for accepting prerecorded audio files. Does the station prefer CDs, DVDs, or audio cartridges? How many audio tracks? What type of file format? Follow each station's requirements faithfully, or be prepared to never hear your recording on the air. Provide exactly what is requested. Keep and periodically update a file of which station wants what. Technological advances and equipment changes at the station can render your information obsolete if you do not keep them up to date.

PUBLIC SERVICE ANNOUNCEMENTS

Public service announcements (PSAs) aired on radio and television are designed to inform and educate, rather than sell a product or service. Because of their educational nature, PSAs are often used for public safety messages that can be presented by an EMS agency. For general-type information such as swimming safety, Halloween costume safety, car seats for children, and crossing streets safely, seek content from state and national organizations dedicated to reducing deaths and injuries in those subject areas.

For local programs and safety-related community events, script and record your own messages specific to the topic and date. Stations air PSAs at no cost during times when they have nothing else to air of a higher priority. Paid commercials and other programming will always take precedence. To improve the chances of having your PSA aired, script three versions—one at 15 seconds long, one at 20 seconds long, and the third at 30 seconds long. Write the 30-second version first in the inverted pyramid style of a news story. Cut from the bottom, eliminating details and time until you reach the two shorter lengths. Read the scripts aloud in a normal speaking voice, editing as needed until the exact times are achieved. Accuracy counts because time is money to the radio station, where 30 seconds means 30 seconds, not 31 or even 30.5.

Community-minded radio stations will let public service agencies record PSAs at no charge in their studio with their own professional engineer operating their equipment to ensure the best possible result. The station may also re-record duplicate copies you can distribute to other stations. Be sure to have

your list of other stations' audio file formats with you.

VIDEO PRESENTATIONS

Digital video technology offers many ways to easily and cost-effectively inform, educate, and capture events for posterity. As with any other technology, ease of use does not necessarily equal the highest quality. Develop a good sense of what is good enough for you in terms of shooting and using video, based on your intended use. Because computer screens display images at a lower resolution than televisions, videos destined for Internet use can be of a much lower resolution than video intended for television.

An important aspect to remember with video is that you are also capturing audio. The same care that goes into recording an audio clip or PSA for radio is necessary when shooting video. Do not rely solely on the camera's built-in microphone. It will do a much better job of capturing any sound from the camera operator than from the subject being videoed.

MAINTAIN RELATIONSHIPS WITH LOCAL TELEVISION

Along with print media and radio, maintain a good personal and professional relationship with television stations that cover your jurisdiction. Depending on the size of the area and population you serve, you may have one or more local stations with which to work. Even communities with no local television station have nearby larger-market stations that want to cover their surrounding communities.

Assignment editors set the rules for contact and submission of materials to the television station. They may assign a producer to you as your personal gatekeeper or send you directly to a news reporter as your primary contact. This contact will determine your primary contact for news stories, PSAs, feature stories, and coverage of community events, much like when you work with radio stations.

In addition to news programming, local affiliates of national networks based in large markets often produce their own programming. These may be weekday talk shows, weekend public service offerings, and local, in-depth documentaries. Become familiar with the programs and hosts to see where you and your agency can be featured. Make yourself available and your interest known.

When asked to be a guest on one of these programs, watch several episodes of the show to become familiar with the host, whether you will be answering questions from anyone besides the host, the format, and whether there is a live studio audience. Prearrange a general outline of the topic or topics to be discussed so you can thoroughly prepare yourself. If you plan to have visual aids, prearrange how to bring them to the program so they will show the most effectively.

USING LOCAL CABLE

When the market area is large enough, cable television providers will offer studio space, engineers, and equipment for community residents and organizations to produce their own local access cable television programs. These programs are broadcast on the cable provider's local access channel to all customers within the geographic region that provider covers.

Creating 30 or 60 minutes of programming for a weekly, biweekly, or even monthly show is a significant undertaking. Research how much effort is involved by watching other local access programs that are similar in content and format to what you want to do. Ask the hosts and the studio technicians to describe their process and the time required

to produce their programs. Decide if you have the time or resources to take on a commitment this large.

PRODUCING YOUR OWN VIDEO

Think of video the same way you would photographs. If you only need a snapshot, then it is probably okay to shoot the video yourself with a decent camera. If you are looking for high-quality images, then hire a video production team. If the video project includes a partner agency or interest in the subject is shared, the partner may be persuaded to share the production costs in exchange for copies of the final product.

Training sessions can be videotaped for future reference and for distribution to outlying stations. Having these training videos on the library shelf mean anyone can at any time grab a video and brush up on their skills. When a new piece of equipment is received, videotape the initial training session so responders who missed the training can catch up.

If your budget does not allow for a professional video production team, entice a local school or scout troop with video capabilities to take on your assignment as a class or merit badge project. You may have veteran amateur or professional videographers in your area who would be willing to respond on call to help document major events. They may offer low- or no-fee work in exchange for the opportunity to get prime access to the excitement.

DISTRIBUTING VIDEOS

Once videos have been made, they can be distributed internally and externally, depending on their purpose and usage. The agency's website is an excellent place to post videos for general internal and external viewing and archival purposes. Be careful not to put anything on your website that is of a confidential nature. Once it goes live, anyone in the world with Internet access can see and pass it along to others.

Burn enough DVDs to distribute training videos to each of your shifts and stations. A lower-cost alternative is to have a secure area on your website that can only be accessed by viewers with an authorized login. This is a way to distribute video widely, yet maintain some control over who has access to it.

If you do plan to provide television stations with your own video clips, PSAs, or other programming pieces, refer to each station's technical specifications for submitted videos. Does the station want DVDs or tape cartridges? Can it accept, or alternately does it prefer, high-definition video files?

■ INTERNET PRESENCE ─────────

Your agency's website is an indispensable tool for keeping your audiences informed and educated. Information can be simultaneously presented when new and archived for future reference, all with one upload. Using the website to its full potential as an informational tool will require a commitment to maintaining the site's content. Your goal for the information on the site is to be able to say "There's more information about that on our website" in answer to nearly any question about the agency and how it operates. Make it a routine part of the job for yourself or your webmaster designee to keep content fresh and accurate.

KEEPING THE AGENCY WEBSITE UP TO DATE

Decide who will keep your website up to date. You may have the budget to hire professional web support for this task. On the other hand, you may have the requisite skills in your own agency to post text, photos, video,

and electronic documents. Do not go more than a week without updating the news section, even if it is only updating year-to-date run statistics.

Try not to go more than one month without reviewing time-sensitive information such as class announcements, scheduled public events, public meeting minutes, and personnel changes. Look for personnel within your agency who can help maintain the site. Even if they do not have the skills to change content, they can do time-sensitive reviews and provide you with a weekly or monthly list of what needs to be added, deleted, and updated.

About the Agency

Your website should be the single-greatest source of information about the agency. Every item, fact, feature, and story related to the agency that can be released for public view can and should be available on your site. Consult with site-design experts to make the site plan, visual experience, and links to navigate through the website as useful as possible. Because the site will contain so much information about many different agency-related subjects, include a search function so viewers with a specific question can find answers quickly and efficiently.

How you categorize information on the site is up to you and your expert design help. There is no single standard to follow. By the nature of an EMS agency's design, a station-by-station site plan is commonly used. Include photos of each station's interior and exterior, equipment, personnel, and public services. When discussing public meeting or classroom spaces, include photos of those rooms in use.

In the About section of the site, include an organization chart and describe how the agency is funded and governed. Publicly owned agencies can post budgets and related financial data to show taxpayers, by line item and graphically in charts, where the agency's income comes from and how it is spent. A young agency's history can be included in the About section. For older, established agencies, make the history portion a section by itself with interesting narrative and archival photos.

Include a recruiting section with full details on every type of position in the agency, whether paid or not, and the educational and experience standards for each. Include an electronic version of the entire application packet for people to view and download. When openings occur in any position, post a job announcement here and in the News section.

News Section

The sections just mentioned get reviewed monthly and require infrequent changes. Where you will spend the most time is keeping the news section very active and frequently updated. The news section is where you will post the following:

* Every press release
* Press conference notes and photos
* Links to local media coverage of the agency
* Every public newsletter
* Action photos with captions
* Video links

When the news items are no longer fresh, usually within a month or so after the initial posting, move them into archives that are labeled to make searches easier.

Links to Media Outlets

Providing links to other related websites adds value for visitors to your website. Create a list of website addresses, also known as Uniform Resource Locaters (URLs), to the media outlets with which you have established relationships. It is considered polite web policy to seek permission first, then exchange URLs with outside websites. Their URL appears as a link on your site, and yours is linked on their site. This increases web visitors to both sites.

Whenever one of your linked media sources features your agency in a story, post a link directly to that story on your site's news page. Check all links every 3 months to ensure continued normal operation. Broken links are frustrating for viewers and diminish the perceived value of your agency.

Links to Stakeholders, Partners, Public Groups

Links to other websites will add valuable content to your site. Create a list of website URLs for each of your stakeholders, partners, and public groups, then seek permission to exchange links. Your site's viewers might want to look up what stakeholders allow for the agency's operations. Prospective responders can use a stakeholder link as a conduit to information on qualifications for different certification or license levels.

Including partner URLs is a nice acknowledgement to them and a reminder to your own personnel that they are a valued asset that helps your agency fulfill its mission every day. The same is true when you add selected public group URLs. When posting links to commercial entities and public-service group sites, add a disclaimer that advises that the link's presence is informational only and does not constitute any endorsement by the agency.

Any favorable mention of your agency in stakeholder, partner, or public group websites can be added by link to your own site's News section. As with any links, periodic testing for continued operation is essential. However, because these types of sites are generally updated less frequently than news media sites, checks only need to be done every 6 months or so.

BLOGS

Similar to writing a column in the local newspaper, starting a **blog** on your agency's website is an opportunity for you and other writers in the agency to address issues influencing, affecting, or interesting to you. By their nature, blogs are written in a more personable style, revealing the insights and opinions of the writer as well as the facts of the topic being discussed. Free online software will let you create attractive blogs, control how the reader's browser displays it, and link it to your website.

Before starting a blog, ask yourself how much time you have to commit to its upkeep. A blog that allows readers to submit comments needs to be moderated to protect your name and site. Before any outside comment can be posted for the world to see, you or your designee must first review it for content to ensure that nothing appears on the agency's site that might reflect badly on the agency, violate laws, or be spam.

Some blog writers send an email blast to subscribers and others to announce when each new blog is posted. Be sure to include an opt-out mechanism in every email so that anyone who does not wish to receive future emails can be taken off your email address list. Failure to offer opt-out functionality, or to honor opt-

out requests, can be annoying to recipients and a violation of the law in some states.

ANNOUNCING WEB AND SOCIAL MEDIA UPDATES

In addition to writing and blasting a blog to subscribers, consider using **really simple syndication (RSS)** technology to announce updates made to your website and the social media sites on which you maintain an agency presence. RSS allows readers to subscribe to news feeds from any site that offers the service. Instead of having periodically check favorite websites for new content, RSS subscribers are alerted by the website whenever content has been updated. Depending on the options provided by the website, the readers can opt to have the RSS feeds sent to their email or other electronic communication methods. RSS feeds are especially helpful to readers who want to monitor websites that do not change frequently or on a regular schedule.

CHAPTER REVIEW

Summary

Messages can be delivered to targeted audiences in a number of written, oral, and electronic ways. EMS managers who can identify the means available to them and select the correct route to an intended audience will be successful in achieving their informational and educational goals for that message. Maintaining current and accurate contact files is a critical step to ensure that messaging routes remain available when needed.

Each messaging delivery route has its strengths and weaknesses. Oral presentations offer significant advantages in making sure your message is understood, but are limited in the number of people you can reach.

Written reports carry in-depth information, but provide no guarantee of being read or understood. Mass media reports offer one-shot reach to masses of people, but may not be seen or read by all your intended targets. The Internet offers a comprehensive blend of written, video, and audio presentations, but requires the audience to find it.

There is no one, single, correct messaging route to everyone. However, by prioritizing what messages are the most important and using the best means of delivering the messages, EMS managers can have an informational and educational impact on their communities.

WHAT WOULD YOU DO? Reflection

Les has reviewed all the message delivery methods available to him and created a catalog divided into oral, written, electronic, and Internet categories. For each category, he has listed the strengths and weaknesses of each delivery method, along with any similarities each has to one another. He also cross-referenced delivery categories with the audience or audiences each would be most useful in reaching.

He found ways to increase and improve informational and educational efforts while reducing his workload and streamlining his message delivery process by identifying where he could use duplication, technology, and agency personnel to his benefit. With just one written document, he can use four distribution outlets to inform massive numbers of people. A single press release can be sent to newspapers, radio stations, television stations, and posted on the agency website with little or no change. By using RSS technology, the reach of a single effort to post on the website is multiplied by the number of RSS subscribers. Providing printed materials and briefing information to responders expands the abilities and number of people engaged in public outreach.

Review Questions

1. For what three reasons should you attend as many stakeholders meetings as possible?
2. Give two examples of when to call a press conference.
3. Koegel uses the acronym OPEN UP to describe the six characteristics of an exceptional presenter. What does OPEN UP stand for?
4. Describe how you would conclude a presentation to a general audience.
5. Brochures can be created and provided for responders to hand out at the right time on appropriate calls. List at least three appropriate topics for such a brochure.
6. What are public service announcements (PSAs) designed to do?
7. When maintaining your agency's website, what should you update on a monthly basis?

Reference

Koegel, Timothy J. (2007) *The Exceptional Presenter.* Greenleaf Book Group Press. Austin, Texas.

Key Terms

blog A contraction of the term *web log* where individuals post ongoing narratives written from their perspective.

Really Simple Syndication (RSS) Technology used to tell subscribers when information on a website has been updated.

sunshine meetings Gatherings held by public agencies that are legally required to be open to public viewing and participation.

Press Releases

Objectives

After reading this chapter, the student should be able to:

8.1 Describe the different reasons and ways to use press releases.
8.2 Discuss the essential elements of a lead.
8.3 Explain the fundamental of clear writing.
8.4 Describe the difference between hard news and features.

Overview

This title identifies and offers examples of the informational and educational components that work together to form a comprehensive public relations plan. Capitalizing on successful strategies used in marketing and advertising, it explains the reasons why public information and education are necessary for gaining and holding the public trust.

Key Terms

announcement press
   releases
boilerplate language

breaking news
inverted pyramid
   style

press releases
writing tight copy

WHAT WOULD YOU DO?

To find the time to write and send more press releases, you must find a way to streamline the writing process.

Source: © buchachon/Fotolia

To meet his public information and education challenges, Les Phillips wants to increase the number and types of press releases he sends out. He realizes he will need to improve his writing skills to accomplish this. First, he needs to craft better documents that are factual, well-written, make them interesting to read, and convey the correct message. Second, he realizes that to find the time to write and send more press releases, he must find a way to streamline the writing process.

Questions

1. How can Les become a better press release writer?
2. How can Les streamline the process to shorten the time required to write a press release?

■ INTRODUCTION

Press releases are an easy and effective way to send information to large numbers of people. Press releases are also cost effective. Your only cost is the time spent writing and sending the release. The mass media bears the effort and cost of distribution for you.

Using press releases effectively begins with knowing what circumstances call for writing a release. The second step is having a solid knowledge of how to write releases properly.

The importance of proper writing skills, including spelling, sentence structure, grammar, and economy of word use cannot be overstated. The better your release is written, the less work the receiving editor needs to do to make it ready to publish and the more likely it will be used. The final step is delivering the release to the correct person at each media outlet before the publishing deadlines.

Previous groundwork done in building relationships with every media outlet that covers your service area pays off when you start sending press releases. First, you know where to send the release. Also, the recipient is more likely to consider a release from and want to help someone with whom they already have a relationship. Now return that consideration and respect by learning to write them well, along with knowing the times and ways to use press releases.

■ USING PRESS RELEASES

Press releases can be used to make news or respond to news reported from another source. When making news, the press release will announce the news and how the sender is involved in the story. For example, a press release about receipt of a new piece of lifesaving equipment sent out by the EMS agency that has acquired the equipment announces the news (new equipment) and how the agency is involved (as the owner/operator).

Press releases sent in response to news reported from another source may be intended to add details left out of the original story, divert responsibility for actions attributed, or take credit where none was offered. Whether or not to send a response-type press release must be considered carefully. Does the new information offered really add pertinent details?

For example, a newspaper story reports on a community meeting called by citizens concerned over how civilian injuries and deaths at a neighborhood house fire were handled by the local fire department. The story relates the events of the day, quotes neighbors at length on what their concerns were, and details the answers offered by the fire chief, who was not there, and the on-scene command officer. The department wants to send a press release to the paper in response to the story to add details.

The following examples illustrate the difference between sending additional information versus offering pertinent details that add value to the reader:

Example A

Also in attendance at the meeting was Seneca Hammond, EMS Chief of the Colonial Fire Department, who answered questions about patient care.

Example B

In response to questions from the audience, Colonial Fire Department EMS Chief Seneca Hammond gave a 10-minute presentation outlining the actions taken by agency personnel that day and the protocols that guide patient care performed by emergency medical responders. After the meeting, two of the most vocal audience members said Hammond's explanations had answered all their questions.

Example A merely adds a name to the list of who was present. Example B adds pertinent

details about who was there, what they did or said, and what effect they had.

Another consideration for whether or not to send a response-type press release is the question of whether the new information is perceived as self-serving rather than informational. In Example C, the agency's press release appears to take all the glory without adding substance:

Example C

The details of the accident as reported in yesterday's paper failed to note the contributions to overall command and patient care by two of this agency's first responders.

If you read between the lines of Example D, it appears the agency is performing damage control by pointing out its responders were being led by others:

Example D

Agency responders who were on scene due to a mutual aid request were working under the command of an outside agency, which was wholly responsible for the patient outcomes at the tragic, triple-fatality accident.

Be sure the news made by your press release is only the news you intended the press release to make. Poorly chosen words, irrelevant details, or important information omitted can become the story, whether in a press release making news or a response-type release. Avoid inadvertent news making by writing clearly and with your informational goal always in mind.

BREAKING STORIES

What is the difference between **breaking news** and an announcement? Both can use press releases to convey information. A sense of timing and relative importance of the information are key determining factors. *Breaking news* is a familiar term to anyone who watches television newscasts. In the television news world, a combination of timing plus relative importance deems a story breaking news. In the world of press releases, relative importance mostly defines the difference between breaking news and announcements. Split-second timing is rarely a factor; however, a day or two difference in when the information publishes can be important.

A breaking news press release is important, new information from the agency that you want to reach the public as soon as possible. Examples could be the appointment of a new chief, election results, major changes in how the agency operates, annual run statistics, or new facilities.

Breaking news can also be a response-type release to news that is being reported by other sources and currently commanding high levels of attention from the media and public. In this context, timing does matter as much as relative importance. When you are presenting additional facts or rebutting false information, you must do so while the topic is on readers' minds, or they may never notice your clarifications.

ANNOUNCEMENTS

Announcement press releases offer information on routine agency business such as meetings, classes, special events, and special accomplishments. Although still important, these types of topics are not considered to be as newsworthy as breaking news. Announcements of upcoming events should be sent out at least a week before deadlines, giving the media time to publish at their convenience. Do not send announcement press releases with short deadlines unless you have no choice because a detail changes at the last minute.

FEATURES

Features differ from hard news by their emphasis on the human and emotional aspects of a story. The facts of the story remain the same, but features add elements that make the reader become more intimately involved with the persons and events in the story.

A hard news story about the agency receiving its first 100-percent score on a state inspection would start like this:

ACME EMS earned the first perfect, 100-percent score in its history on the state Department of Health's quarterly inspection last week.

A feature story about the same event would start like this:

When ACME EMS Chief Dan Banner was hired last year, he vowed to bring the agency up to the same high standards he had achieved in neighboring Columbia County. In just 11 months, he has exceeded his promise with ACME improving from an average of 49 percent to the first perfect 100-percent score in its history on the state Department of Health's quarterly inspection last week.

Features can be distributed as press releases but are less commonly done than hard news and announcements. Features are constructed in a manner different from hard news and contain more than just hard facts. Read features to learn how they are written and what types of information they contain. Unless you are an accomplished writer, you may want to send feature stories to media outlets as outlined suggestions for their own reporters to follow up on.

Feature outlines can be sent in conjunction with the related breaking news press release, inviting media outlets to further explore the human aspects of the story on their readers' behalf. As an example, here is the beginning of a breaking news press release, along with suggestions for a companion feature story:

Manchester High School Football Coach Bill Wood was revived by Manchester EMS after suffering a heart attack and collapsing on the sidelines during last night's championship game. The EMS crew was on standby duty in the end zone in case of player injuries and was able to render aid to the coach immediately.

The story continues with all the details of the event and the coach's current condition. At the end of the press release is the following suggestion for an accompanying feature:

[Both paramedics who saved Coach Wood's life grew up in Manchester and played four years of football under his coaching. They both have strong feelings to share about their experience last night and credit the coach's teachings about teamwork for being able to work together so well when he collapsed. They can be reached through this office.]

INVERTED PYRAMID CONSTRUCTION

A pyramid has a small top, held up by an all-important broad base. How big the base can be is dependent on how much room is available to build the pyramid. The top layers can be left off and the pyramid will still stand.

News stories have an all-important broad base: the main facts of the story. Less important details can be left out and the story will still stand, or do its job of reporting the key facts. Stories also have space limitations on how long the story can be, based on how much other news and advertising fit on the page in newspapers, and how much time remains after commercials and other news in radio and television. Even Internet-based news has limitations based on what fits with other news and ads within a single browser frame on a computer screen.

For a news story to stand, even with elements removed, the broad base must come first. (See Figure 8.1.) This is known in journalism as writing in the **inverted pyramid style**. The most important information appears in the first paragraph, also known as the lead. As the story progresses, more information is presented in descending order of importance to the overall story. Writing a story in this manner means cuts made from the bottom of the story remove detail, but the most important information will always be retained.

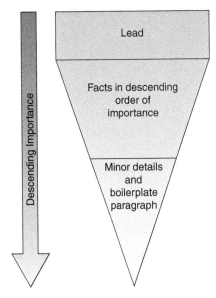

FIGURE 8.1 ■ In the inverted pyramid style of news writing, information is presented in descending order of importance to the overall story.

Write press releases in the inverted pyramid style. The best press releases can be published with little to no effort on the editor's part. When your press releases look the same in the paper as they do when you sent them, you have written a professional release and earned respect from the editor.

BOILERPLATE LANGUAGE

All press releases need to include certain types of repetitious information known collectively as **boilerplate language**. The advantage of using boilerplate language is that the information is always included, is always correct, and is always presented in the same way to prevent confusion.

Press releases contain at least four different pieces of boilerplate: release date, expiration date, information contact, and agency description. The first three are placed outside the text at the top of the press release. The agency description boilerplate describes the agency and is the final paragraph in the inverted pyramid style text. Here is an example of last-paragraph agency boilerplate:

The Cooks Hill Fire Department (CHFD) provides basic and advanced life support emergency medical services to 18,000 residents over 180 square miles in and around the city of Cooks Hill. With two staffed stations and six volunteer stations, CHFD responds to nearly 4,000 9-1-1 calls for emergency medical help each year.

Consistent boilerplate usage allows creation and use of templates that speed up the process of creating press releases. Start a document using your word processing software. Insert imagery from your agency's letterhead to make the document appear as if it were written on agency letterhead. Start with today's date, followed by a double-space return. The next line should read *Release Date:* followed by the first day the information can appear in the media. This date is determined by the content of the press release. The most common release date is *Immediately.*

After another double-space return, the next line should read *Use until,* followed by a date. This is to prevent old news from being printed. In the case of an announcement of a class to be held on May 25, you would write *Use until May 24* on this line. After another double-space return, type *For More Information Contact:* followed by the name, phone number, and email address of the person to be called with any questions about the release's contents.

Next on the template, create a space for the headline, followed by a place to start the first paragraph of the press release text. Finally, type in the boilerplate agency information as the past paragraph.

Here is another example of boilerplate agency information:

LongLife EMS provides emergency medical services in the City of Waterview and the surrounding communities throughout Columbia County. As the primary 9-1-1 emergency response agency, LongLife

EMS operates five paramedic ambulances from three stations on about 22,000 emergency medical calls per year.

With this template saved, each succeeding press release is already properly formatted and ready to fill in new details. This reduces effort, saves time, and ensures all pertinent data are included on every press release.

■ WRITING LEADS

A journey of a thousand miles start with one step. A press release starts with one word. At times, it seems both can be equally daunting. The first paragraph of a news story is the lead, and in its own way a press release. A good lead introduces readers to the story with enough information to decide whether to continue reading. Is the story pertinent to their lives, does it look interesting, does it seem entertaining, or is the subject something they care nothing about?

Your press release lead must answer all those questions in just a handful of words that also include all the main facts of the story. In the inverted pyramid style of writing, even if everything else in the story is cut from the bottom up, the lead will contain enough information to tell the essential facts of the story. Writers can agonize over leads, or they can use templates and practice over and over until leads seem to write themselves.

ESSENTIAL INGREDIENTS

All leads contain the essential facts of the story:

+ Who is the story about, or who is presenting the story?
+ What is the story about?
+ Where does the story take place?
+ When does the story happen?
+ Why is the story news, or why is the event in the story happening?
+ How do the events of the story unfold?

Leads answer these questions in as few words as possible in order to gain the readers' attention. If too many words are used, the reader may not be hooked immediately, will get bored, and will move on to another story. At the same time, if key details are missing, the reader can get confused and will move on to another story.

ECONOMY OF WORDS

Writing a good lead in requires a fine balance: providing as much information as possible in as few words as possible. In journalism, that is known as **writing tight copy**. The text is loaded with information without the use of no extraneous words. The following three examples are drafts of leads written for the same press release:

Example A
Cascades EMS Chief Sue Thomas said authorities have called off the search being launched from Cascades Trailhead number 27 for two hikers, Bob and Jane Peterson, who were reported missing three days ago on Mount Bachelor by their children, Bob Jr., Jeanelle, and Francis, because of weather conditions.

Example B
The search for two missing hikers will not begin until weather conditions improve.

Example C
Authorities announced today that the search for two hikers who have been missing on Mount Bachelor for three days cannot start until whiteout snow conditions subside.

At 48 words, Example A is too long to read in a glance and contains far too many details about locations, the hikers' names, and children's names, without explaining why the weather was responsible. Example B is too cryptic, failing to say who made the announcement, where the hikers are, how long they have been missing, or why the weather is a factor.

Example C uses just 25 words to fully detail:

* Who (authorities announce, missing hikers)
* What (search suspended)
* Where (Mount Bachelor)
* When (announced today, missing three days)
* Why (whiteout snow conditions)
* How (missing three days, searched for one-day so far).

PAINT A PICTURE WITH WORDS

A good lead will form a picture in readers' minds as if they were right there, looking at the event being described. Write your lead, close your eyes, and picture what you have just described. Show the lead to someone else and have them describe the image of what you've painted with your words. Is it an accurate description of what you meant to portray?

Painting a picture does not mean describing every item in painstaking detail. That works in a novel or in a scientific paper, but there is no room or need to be so inclusive in a press release lead. Only include the necessary facts. Give the reader's imagination a little credit for being able to fill in some details.

Side Bar

Examples of Painting a Picture

Too wordy:

Two people were injured in a T-bone collision between a green Chevrolet $\frac{3}{4}$-ton pickup with a canopy and a blue 2008 Toyota Sienna van at the intersection of 27th Street and Grand Avenue Friday afternoon.

Better:

Two people were injured when a pickup truck and small van collided at the intersection of 27th Street and Grand Avenue Friday afternoon.

For an example, the detailed specifics of the type of collision and exactly what kind of vehicles belong further down in the press release. The color of the vehicles is really only relevant if it was a hit-and-run and police were seeking help finding the car. Let the reader's imagination fill in some of the details in a thorough, yet tightly written lead. One vehicle versus another at an intersection is all the picture you need include in the lead so the reader can decide if he or she is interested in reading further.

Best Practice

Best Practices for EMS Press Releases

Sam Bradley, BS, EMT-P

1. Assure that the recipient knows the release is coming from an "official" source and is, therefore, accurate. Assure the recipient has identification and contact information for that person.
2. Assure the release is well written or it may be disregarded for one that is.
3. Identify the audience the press release is intended for: general public, print media, video media, internet, etc.
4. Use the basic rules of journalism to assure all the information is included:
   a. Who
   b. What
   c. Where
   d. When
   e. Why
   f. How
5. Give journalists just facts and the hard data that your product, service, or news is accurate and worth paying attention to.
6. Start with a "hook" that will interest them in the news, then provide a simple, concise picture while keeping confidentiality. The first ten words are the most effective.
7. Be careful not to use industry jargon that may not be understood by your target audience.
8. Make sure the release it edited before submission.

HEADLINES

Every press release needs a headline positioned directly above the lead, just as it will appear in the newspaper. Editors will expect to see one on the press release, even though they may change it before publishing the story. The fact that it is there shows your professional approach to writing a proper press release.

The difference between a headline and a title is use of a verb. Headlines convey action and require a verb. *Two Motorists Injured* is a headline. *Two Injuries* is a title. *Man Suffers Cardiac Arrest in Store* is a headline. *Cardiac Arrest at Store* is a title. News stories always use headlines. Titles are reserved for editorials, commentaries, and features. (See Figure 8.2.)

Headlines are nearly always written in the present or future tense. Readers are more interested in what is happening now or in the future than something that appears to already be over. Even when the reader knows the story is about a past event, seeing a present-tense

Cooks Hill Fire Department
EMS Division
2812 Defib Drive, Cooks Hill, WA 98531

January 12, 2013

FOR IMMEDIATE RELEASE

For more information, contact:

Les Phillips   1-360-555-5555
                        EMSDivChief@chfd.ems

Cooks Hill FD Receives Grant Funding for New Medic Unit

The Cooks Hill Fire Department (CHFD) has received $175,000 in grant funding from local lumber giant Van Dyke Timber Company to help purchase and equip a new medical response unit.

Van Dyke Timber president, Scott Van Dkye, said, "Our company has been in this town for generations. Our local fire department and medics have always been very important and given top-notch service to us. But last month when they saved the life of my grandfather and company founder, well, that made it personal. This is just our way of saying thank you."

Cooks Hill EMS Division Chief Les Phillips said, "This most generous grant from the Van Dyke company is most appreciated. It will allow us to replace the oldest medic unit in our fleet now when it should be done, not in five years when we could have saved up enough money."

A committee has been formed at CHFD to draw up specifications and plans to have the unit ordered and delivered within six months.

"One of the first decisions the committee made was to make sure Van Dyke Timber will be acknowledged on the new unit for all the world to see," Phillips said.

Founded in 1922, Cooks Hill Fire Department provides fire protection and emergency medical services to 180 square miles in and around the city of Cooks Hill, Washington. With 51 employees and 37 volunteers, CHFD responds to nearly 4,000 9-1-1 calls for service each year. Approximately 70 percent of those calls are for emergency medical services.

FIGURE 8.2 ■ Sample press release.

headline will still make it seem more interesting. *New Chief Starts Job* sounds more interesting and engaging than *New Chief Started Job*. The former focuses on the new chief and entices the reader to read on. By being past tense, the word *Started* says the story is already over and closes the door to further exploration.

The purpose of a headline is to draw the reader's eye and announce what the story below is about. Like the lead, it needs to convey the essence of the story in a hurry, using a fraction of the number of words in the lead. Headlines cannot include every detail in the lead, so use them to capture the most important or most interesting detail out of the lead.

Side Bar

Examples of Headlines

EMS Agency Earns 100% Score

ACME EMS earned the first perfect, 100-percent score in its history on the state Department of Health's quarterly inspection last week.

Coach Survives Heart Attack

Manchester High School Football Coach Bill Wood was revived by Manchester EMS after suffering a heart attack and collapsing on the sidelines during last night's championship game. The EMS crew was on standby duty in the end zone in case of player injuries and was able to render aid to the coach immediately.

In the following example, some might be tempted to say *Missing Hikers,* but the extra word is not needed. Why would there be a search if they were not missing?

Search Suspended for Hikers

Authorities announced today they have suspended the one-day search for two hikers missing on Mount Bachelor for three days until whiteout snow conditions subside.

Collision Injures Two

Two people were seriously injured when a pickup truck and small van collided at the intersection of 27th Street and Grand Avenue Friday afternoon.

Some writers start with the headline as the most important detail, and then expand it to write the lead with additional pertinent facts. Others write the lead, then choose which fact to make important enough to star in the headline. The correct method is to use what you prefer as long as it produces a quality headline and lead.

■ CLEAR WRITING

Writing clearly and concisely is a learned skill. Just like any other learned skill, writing well takes training and continuous practice. Formal training is available in local colleges. Independent-study training can be found in self-help books. Informal training is available all around you just by reading others' writing in newspapers.

Make it a habit to read as much material as possible similar to what you want to write. Read multiple newspapers as often as you can. Use the Internet to read leading newspapers online. If your press releases read like stories in major metropolitan daily newspapers, you are writing high-quality press releases.

You may receive press releases at your agency. Often organizations will write one press release and send it not only to media outlets, but also to other organizations they want to reach. Use these releases as exercises to evaluate the template, boilerplate, headline, lead, and inverted pyramid content. By evaluating and rewriting better versions as needed, you are practicing the art of writing clear, concise press releases.

NO WASTED WORDS

Clear writing means leaving out words that do not add content or context to the story being told. If they do not move the story along, they are wasting space and cluttering up the narrative.

The following two examples show how the same information can be written using one-third fewer words:

Example A
If, on the other hand, the levy is not passed, seven employees will be given layoff notices and service levels will be reduced by as much as 20 percent.

Example B
If the levy does not pass, seven employees will be laid off and service reduced up to 20 percent.

Example B uses 19 words to say the same thing as Example A does in 29 words. The extra words in Example A are all qualifiers and fillers that take up space and add nothing to the facts of the story.

In Example C, the sentence stretches for 35 words when only 16 are needed to tell the same story:

Example C
Paramedics were called to the street in front of a small, brown house on East Maple Street where they cared for a woman who was sitting on the curb crying and bleeding from the face.

How can we pare down the 35 words used in Example C? *Paramedics were called to* is not needed because the reader already knows paramedics go where they are called. *The street in front of a small brown house* does nothing to tell what happened. *Where they cared for* uses four words to say *treated. Sitting on the curb* is more irrelevant information.

The important elements of this story can be told in just 16 words: *Paramedics treated a woman on East Maple Street who was crying and bleeding from the face.*

Adjective phrases built with prepositions are another area where words are often wasted. Anytime you start to write *of the something* or *on the something* after a noun, stop and try rewriting the sentence by putting *something* before the noun. You will save two words and make the sentence flow better.

By not wasting words, you engage and increase readers' interest by letting them do some of the work. *It was raining when the collision occurred just after midnight.* With just these words, the reader will imagine a scene with cars crashed on a dark, wet street with poor visibility and slippery conditions. If the exact scene details are not important to the story, let readers engage their imagination and participate in the story as they read.

ACTION VERBS

Verbs set the tempo of a story. They add action, interest, and enthusiasm. Is the story a dull recitation or an interesting description of an event? *Community members attended the meeting* versus *Community members filled the meeting room.* Does the reader's pulse increase along with the tempo of the story? *Paramedics responded to help the victim* versus *Paramedics rushed to save the victim.* Does the story elicit sympathy for its primary character? *The woman asked for help as she looked at the river* versus *The woman cried out for help while scanning the river with her eyes.* The difference shown in each example lies in the choice of action words used. Both sentences convey the same facts, but in a different rhythm and emotional tempo.

Use verbs wisely to add to the story's tempo, but be careful not to substitute verbs that express the same action in vastly different ways. Even in something as simple as attributing a quote, the writer can convey an entirely different picture of the conversation. Was it something the speaker said, cried, yelled, screamed, shouted, or whispered? Each verb refers to the use of language, but in entirely different ways. Did the cars hurtle, crash, slam, collide, tap, or bump into each other? Each verb elicits a different concept of the speed and force of the collision. You would never call a blue house red because it is not accurate. Similarly, do not use hurtle

---

Side Bar

Common Examples of Tighter Writing

chief of the agency	agency chief
chairman of the board	board chairman
lights on the ambulance	ambulance lights
report of the committee	committee report
report on absenteeism	absenteeism report

or slam to describe action at a simple fender bender.

Along with powerful verbs comes the temptation to increase their emphasis by adding adverbs. Adverbs can add nuance; however, they can also introduce your interpretation or opinion into the story. Although some interpretation may be inevitable as you relate facts, opinions never belong in a news release. *The man shouted angrily from the crowd.* How do you know he was angry? Was it his words or the tone of his voice? On the other hand, did he just shout in order to be heard over the noise of the crowd? If you are not sure of the facts and the additional description is not central to the story, then leave adverbs out.

STAND-ALONE NOUNS

Be sparing with adjectives. Whenever possible in your writing, let nouns stand on their own to identify persons, places, or things. Sometimes adjectives are not even needed. *The big, red fire truck was parked blocking the traffic lane where paramedics were working when it was struck by a small car.* Adding *big* and *red* to describe the fire truck contributes nothing to the essential facts of the story, and they are unnecessary details in a community where all fire trucks are big and red.

The tall, burly paramedic struggled to extricate the patient from her compact car. If the story is about the difficulties tall or burly rescuers face when working in and around small cars, the adjectives may be appropriate. If the story is about the crash and how the patient needed extrication, descriptors for the paramedic are irrelevant.

Adjectives can be used appropriately when they help paint a picture central to the facts of the story. *The petite woman was injured in the collision.* The adjective petite adds nothing of value to the reader's understanding. *The petite woman was easily extricated from her car.*

Now the adjective helps describe the reason she was easily extricated.

Be careful using modifiers that are vague, inaccurate, or can be defined vastly differently by people. Your definition of *old* will be different from someone who is 20 years older or 20 years younger than you. Use the actual age, if appropriate, or let the noun stand alone if age is not pertinent to the story. *The patient was revived by paramedics after he suffered a massive heart attack.* Why use the word massive here? Was his heart the size of a basketball? Would *serious* be a better adjective? Alternatively, why not leave the adjective out and let readers fill in their own notion of what kind of heart attack requires revival?

Adjectives can lure you down the same dangerous paths as adverbs by inadvertently adding your opinion to the story. *An external investigation of the agency has concluded that the outrageous claims made by Mrs. Parker had no merit.* None of your readers would be surprised to see that you disagree with Mrs. Parker, but that does not give you the right to say so in your press release. If this was a direct quote from an agency authority, then the adjective could remain as long as it was attributed to the person who said it:

Commissioner Richard Wong said, "An external investigation of the agency has concluded that the outrageous claims made by Mrs. Parker had no merit."

Adjectives can also be misused by modifying the wrong noun in the sentence. *The reckless car struck four parked cars before the driver finally came to a rest against the supermarket.* The car was not reckless. If anything was reckless, it would have been the driver.

USING QUOTES

Quotes add interest, help substantiate facts through expert testimony, and offer a chance to introduce opinions of key players in the story being told. Adding these elements without attributing them to another source makes the writer their owner. Although the writer may agree with what is being said, he or she is responsible for making sure that there is no misunderstanding by attributing statements and opinions to their rightful owners.

This quote adds interest to a press release about a recently concluded public education class: *Class attendee Michele Van Dyke said, "I signed up for this CPR and first aid class because I have my first child on the way and I want to be able to handle any emergency."* By including this quote, the writer identifies its owner and offers readers a reason to consider enrolling in the next class.

This quote offers expert testimony to substantiate facts: *EMS Liaison John Guard of the state Department of Health reviewed the report and said, "From what I read in the report, it appears all actions taken were consistent with state law and industry best practices."* To state this without attribution would mean the writer has done the reviewing and concluding, not the state official.

"We believe the proposed budget cuts will seriously impact this agency's ability to provide the kind of quality care our community expects and deserves," EMS Chief Gordon warned. This is a serious expression of opinion that was correctly attributed to someone in authority within the agency. However, there are two words that may cause the writer some problems if left in. The quote starts with the pronoun *we*, then is attributed to a single person. The reader is confused if *we* means the chief is speaking for the agency as a whole, or a group of people on which he is part. It would be better to use *I* here unless *we* gets defined immediately before or after the quote.

The second problematic word is the verb *warned*. Does this mean the chief is predicting the future, delivering an ultimatum, or simply speaking seriously? Unless the writer can define and defend using *warned*, a better choice of verbs would be *said*.

CLICHÉS

Using clichés in a hard news press release is only appropriate if they appear in attributed quotes. Otherwise, try to avoid these signs of lazy writing. Clichés clutter up otherwise clean copy by taking the attention off the story and shouting, "Look at me!" Although the writer may have thought the cliché was clever, the reader is likely to move on quickly to another story.

Clichés may have some use in features to help set the stage for the story to be told. *They say you can't teach an old dog new tricks, but tonight retired local veterinarian James Craig will graduate from Emergency Medical Technician training at age 72.*

FEATURE STORIES

Feature stories can be described as the human news behind the hard news. They explore the why and how people get involved something. Hard news leaves readers feeling informed. Feature stories leave readers feeling emotional, like they have just experienced the same trials or triumphs as the focus of the feature.

PURPOSE

Features can stand on their own, but they are often a sidebar to add important human elements to a news story. A hard news press release about the retirement of a long-time responder would include date started, length of service, milestones in the responder's career, and future plans. An accompanying feature story would include why he entered the profession, have him relate stories in his own words, explore how his years of service have affected him and his outlook on life, and offer his words of wisdom for those who remain on the job.

CONSTRUCTION

Feature stories are written in a circular path. Reading through the story will seem like you have been listening to a friend relate an experience over the phone. The first paragraph is less structured and inclusive than a news story lead; it introduces the reader to the central character or characters and offers a glimpse of where the story will go, as in the following example:

When Lawrence Allen filled out an application to join the Ross Community Ambulance Corps, little did he realize that this new volunteer opportunity would become the main direction of the rest of his life.

Features tend to be written in chronological order. You are not concerned about listing facts in order of importance. Your goal is to tell the story as it happened, one step at a time. At times the first paragraph refers to present day, then the story goes back in time to the beginning, as shown in the next example:

As Lawrence Allen looked back on his 42 years of service to the Ross Community Ambulance Corps, he knew he was ending an important part of his life and worried whether his future would hold enough excitement for him. When Lawrence filled out his application, little did he realize then how much this new volunteer opportunity would affect his life and so many others in the community.

Despite being written in a unique structure, features depend on correct facts and accurate details as much as hard news. What happened to the subject? How have experiences affected him or her? What is the result of these experiences? Personalize the story even more by adding in the person's own words when you can. What you cannot add are opinions unless they have been attributed directly to a person in the story. In the following example, you see personalization and opinion from the story's central character and another person. They are presented in quotes so the reader knows who is relating the experience and to whom the opinions belong:

Lawrence said one of the most difficult calls he remembers was the morning someone reported an abandoned baby in a dumpster behind the supermarket. "My heart stopped when I looked down and saw that beautiful, helpless little baby just dumped in the garbage. As soon as I saw her open those blue eyes, I was filled with sorrow and anger and confusion over how anyone could do that," Lawrence said. "Even though the baby survived, that scene and those thoughts haunted me for a long time," he recalled.

"That baby back in 1982 owes its life to Lawrence's skills and dedication. He managed to put his feelings aside and focus on his patient. He's one of the best EMTs in the businesses," according to Lawrence's long-time partner Ed Louis.

A feature's conclusion completes the circle of the story by referring the reader back to the introduction. The conclusion tells the reader "We brought you into this story, told you the story, and now we have to end. However, before you go, here is the next step this person plans to take. Maybe you'll see him around." This example of a conclusion neatly wraps up the story by including Lawrence's past, present, and future:

At the end of his retirement dinner, Lawrence spent a long time shaking hands, giving and receiving hugs, and immersing himself in the friendship, respect, and camaraderie forged over the last 42 years. The next day he would start on a long-denied vacation, followed by working on his golf game. Earlier in the evening he had said he knew it was time to move on, but just for the moment, the rest of his life could wait a few more minutes.

CHAPTER REVIEW

Summary

Mastering the craft of writing and distributing well-written press releases is a significant advantage for the EMS manager looking to inform and educate as many people as possible. Through mass media, a single press release has the potential for distribution to thousands of people. There are no guarantees how many of those people will see or read the resulting story, but what is guaranteed is that nobody will read a release which was never written or submitted.

The more managers do to provide professionally written releases, the more likely their releases will be published. Editors will respect and use releases that follow journalism's rules of story construction. Submit clear, tight copy by being precise with nouns, verbs, adjectives, and adverbs.

Like any other skill mastered in your career, becoming and remaining a good writer require training and continual practice. Read, write, edit, and compare as much as you can. Never stop looking at your own and others' writing to see where it can be improved.

WHAT WOULD YOU DO? Reflection

To improve his writing skills, Les purchased a newswriting textbook and dedicated time every day to reading multiple newspapers in hand and online. For the first time in his life, he became aware of not only what the stories were telling him, but how they were written. Following the guidelines in the newswriting textbook, he practiced writing press releases for two newspaper stories per day until he decided he was comfortable with his new-found skills.

As he became proficient in writing them, his press releases took less time to prepare.

Les streamlined the process even more by creating a collection of templates. A basic press release template started with his agency's letterhead, all the boilerplate information, and space in which to write the release. He also created specialized templates for recurring events such as monthly meetings, public classes, and public blood pressure checks. By simply changing the boilerplate dates and updating dates, times, and locations in the body text, these press releases could be produced and distributed in mere minutes.

Review Questions

1. What is the difference between breaking news and an announcement?
2. Give two examples of breaking news.
3. How do feature stories differ from hard news?
4. Draw an inverted pyramid as it relates to a news story and explain how it works.
5. What elements does a good lead include?
6. What can quotes do to improve a press release or article?

References

Cappon, Rene J. (2000). *The Associated Press Guide to News Writing,* 3rd ed. Lawrenceville, NJ: Peterson's.

Standring, Suzette Martinez. (2008). *The Art of Column Writing.* Oak Park, IL: Marion Street Press.

Key Terms

announcement press releases Used to distribute information to the public about routine agency business such as meetings, classes, special events, and special accomplishments.

boilerplate language Titles and information that do not change from one press release to the next, in particular the release date, expiration date, information contact, and agency description.

breaking news Information that is deemed immediately newsworthy due to its content and timing.

inverted pyramid style Type of story construction where details are presented in descending order of importance from top to bottom in the story.

press releases Information sent to news media that can be used to make news or respond to news reported from another source.

writing tight copy Providing as many pertinent details as possible while simultaneously using as few words as possible.

Create an Information Culture in Your Agency

9 CHAPTER

Objectives

After reading this chapter, the student should be able to:

9.1 Describe the elements of a public relations (PR) plan.
9.2 Discuss ways to empower agency personnel to participate in the PR plan.
9.3 Explain how to assess the impacts that strategies and actions have on the plan's success

Overview

This title identifies and offers examples of the informational and educational components that work together to form a comprehensive public relations plan. Capitalizing on successful strategies used in marketing and advertising, it explains the reasons why public information and education are necessary for gaining and holding the public trust.

Key Terms

active observers

public relations (PR) plan

speaker's bureau
strategies

WHAT WOULD YOU DO?

You need to decide what message you want to send before you start your campaign.
Courtesy of Estero Fire Rescue.

When Cooks Hill Fire Department EMS Division Chief Les Phillips considered all the different public information and education topics he would like to address, he came to the conclusion that there was more to be done than he could manage by himself along with his other duties. He also realized that if he was the only person engaging in outreach efforts, there would be countless outreach opportunities missed. He decided to look into using other personnel from his agency to help him deliver public information and education messages. However, before he could start recruiting, he needed to define just what his messaging needs and opportunities were.

Questions

1. How can Les define and prioritize his PR activities for his own and others' reference?
2. How can he enlist public outreach support from others in the agency?

■ INTRODUCTION

Nearly every operation at all levels within an EMS agency involves teamwork. Teams of providers do patient care. Crews place the vehicles that carry them to the patient in service each day. A team of professional educators provides initial and ongoing crew training. The agency operates under the guidance of a management team. Considering a team effort in order to implement a public relations plan should come as no surprise to EMS managers.

Having everyone interact with the public in your **public relations (PR) plan** creates an information culture in your EMS agency. Follow the teachable moments training concept, where more experienced responders recognize and seize opportunities to pass on information to less experienced responders. Give agency management, staff, and responders the opportunities, information, and training to be able to recognize teachable moments in their interactions with the public. Your entire agency will work as a team to improve public information and education efforts and help you fulfill your PR program.

■ TOOLS FOR SUCCESS

Success in any profession is the result of having and using the right tools to augment your personal knowledge and skills. Resuscitation of a patient in cardiac arrest requires many tools, including the vehicle that takes you to the scene, the protocols and procedures followed, airway adjuncts, a cardiac monitor and defibrillator, a bag valve mask and oxygen bottle. Teaching a class depends on tools like the curriculum, a computer and projection system, and textbooks.

A successful PR plan depends on a well-crafted public relations strategy to guide all participants towards achieving the agency's public information and education goals. The PR plan is an indispensable tool that offers goals, guidance, budgetary constraints, and benchmarks for measuring success.

DEFINE YOUR AUTHORITY

In establishing and maintaining an information culture within your agency, you will be making decisions that affect how agency staff are trained and the scope of the work they do. You will also have financial needs for personnel and materials costs required to operate an agency-wide public information and education program. You will need a clear understanding of what personnel and financial authority you have to engage in these activities. Along with the authority, you also need to define how much autonomy you have. In other words, do you have the authority to engage any agency personnel and spend any budgeted money on your own, or do you need to present an outline to a superior for approval before each project? Perhaps there is a middle ground instead where you only have to seek project-specific approval if you exceed a certain dollar amount. This authority and autonomy may come from a superior officer, or from the agency's governing board. Whichever the source, obtain permissions in writing that clearly state the boundaries within which you can work independently.

With your authority and autonomy limits defined, you can now seek out others in the agency to help you conduct public information and education plans. As you enlist help, others will have questions about their roles and the processes followed. With your authority defined, you can freely answer to the limits of your autonomy. Knowing who they can

get answers from will make agency personnel more comfortable stepping up to help.

PUBLIC RELATIONS PLAN

Before you effectively conduct any public outreach, draft and have approved a PR plan. This plan is the most important tool for success in a comprehensive, multifaceted PR program. Successful companies draft and follow marketing plans that outline how to reach their targeted audiences in order to sell goods and services. A PR plan can follow the same model. The only real difference is that instead of selling a product to consumers, the EMS agency is distributing information to the public. Just like a marketing plan, general and specific target audiences are identified in the plan. An EMS agency's general public audience is everyone within the agency's response area. Identify subsets of targeted audiences in each of the plan's goals.

The plan directs all efforts by all participants. It commits agency resources and funds, so be sure it is approved at the proper level within your agency. Once approved, you should be able to follow the plan without further need to check in with your superiors. At that point, the plan also becomes the guidebook to answer participants' procedural questions. If the plan is successful, follow-up with superiors will be in the form of after-action reports. If the plan requires changes during its lifetime, follow-up with superiors will be defined by how much authority you have been granted. You may be able to make changes yourself, or you may need a combination of reports and requests to superiors to approve specific structural and budgetary elements.

Public Information and Education Projects

A good PR plan is written for a 12-month period and includes ongoing efforts, specific projects that reoccur on a regular basis, and

Best Practice

National estimates show that one-third of Americans with high blood pressure are unaware of their condition, and another third do not adequately treat it. In addition, an estimated 67 million Americans have undiagnosed type II diabetes. Each year EMS providers in King County, Washington, see approximately 7 percent of the population in King County. This provides responders with opportunities to help identify and control these two health care issues before they become major problems for the patient.

The Supporting Public Health with Emergency Responders (SPHERE) program was created to prevent future 9-1-1 calls by identifying potentially life-threatening conditions whenever a patient is seen by responders. A pilot program was launched in 2006 with two King County fire departments participating. When EMTs assessed patients with abnormally high blood pressure or blood sugar readings, they offered the patient an alert card about the risks of elevated pressure or blood sugar. The card offered information and urged the patient to seek follow-up care. Free follow-up checks at fire stations were also offered. Responders noted who received

alert cards on patient care reports. More than 250 alert cards were handed out in the 9-month pilot period, with 86 percent going to individuals with hypertension.

About 4 weeks after the initial EMS response, the patients were called to see what steps they had taken for their health. Most remembered receiving the alert card, and more than half had sought follow-up care. Two-thirds reported getting their blood pressure checked again. Eighty-five percent reported a positive reaction to being given the alert card.

EMS personnel who participated in the pilot program were also interviewed. An overwhelming majority supported the program and found no problems incorporating the SPHERE program into their normal patient care routines.

The SPHERE program was made part of the King County EMT patient care protocols in 2007, and today all county EMS agencies are participating. SPHERE designers are encouraged by the potential for public health benefits as well as lowering hazards and expense to responders by reducing call volumes.

first-time projects that may or may not happen again. As you add projects or events to the plan, categorize them by type.

Examples of *ongoing* efforts include the following:

+ Knowing when to call 9-1-1
+ Signs and symptoms of a heart attack
+ Signs and symptoms of a stroke
+ Senior fall prevention
+ Child bicycle helmets
+ Healthy lifestyle choices
+ Healthy eating choices
+ Agency and individual awards and recognition
+ New equipment and capabilities
+ Leadership changes
+ Incident follow-ups

Examples of *recurring* efforts include the following:

+ New Year's Eve safety
+ Fourth of July safety
+ Summertime water safety
+ Seasonal outdoor environmental safety
+ Allergy season drugged driving
+ Community festivals and health fairs
+ Public first aid classes
+ Public CPR classes
+ Responder recruitment

Examples of *first-time* events include the following:

+ Co-location with partner agencies' events
+ Funding outreach

* New facility open house
* New community event
* Any new opportunity that may arise

Each project or event in the plan should have the following clearly defined:

* Targeted audience
* Purpose
* Goal
* Strategies to accomplish the goal
* Performance and deadline benchmarks to measure success of strategies en route to achieving the goal
* Budget
* Primary responsible person within the agency.

Your PR plan is a living document, designed to be changeable as conditions warrant. Non-recurring projects that have had their goals achieved can be removed and their resources reassigned to other projects. As progress toward project goals is measured, strategies can be changed to improve lagging performance. New projects can be added, and personnel can be added or changed at any time as well.

Strategies to Accomplish Project Goals

Strategies comprise the step-by-step process that takes each project from inception to fulfillment of its goal. Public outreach strategies can include using the media, speaking engagements, staging public events, sending direct mail, electronic information distribution, and buying newspaper ads. Each strategy requires methods, funding, and effort to implement. For example, a direct mail strategy requires writing copy, designing the piece, printing, developing a mailing list, and mailing. Be aware that accomplishing several of these steps requires spending money with outside sources. A speaking engagement requires writing the presentation, arranging the venue, possibly taking reservations, giving the presentation, and follow-up with audience members as requested. In your plan, you can include

as much or as little detail as you deem necessary on suggested or desired methods used to implement each strategy.

Budget

Determining your PR plan budget starts with knowing how many total dollars are available, and the various sources of those dollars. Depending on where the money comes from, you may be limited in what those funds can be spent on. As an example, you may be able to spend public funds on informational materials regarding an upcoming vote, but not be able to say how you want people to vote. Grant funds may have restrictions on the types of programs or activities they can be used for. Unrestricted funds allow you to use them in any way you like to help achieve your project goals.

Once you have developed a complete list of the information and education projects you want to employ in your 12-month plan, it is time to start determining how much money will be needed to accomplish the goal of each project. Try to anticipate all types and amounts for these expenses, including the following:

* Staff support before, during, and after an event
* Staff support for ongoing outreach projects
* Personnel involved in the project
* Materials and consumables to support the project
* Travel
* Postage and shipping
* Equipment
* Items to be given away

Once you have established budgets for every project in your PR plan, add them all to calculate a grand total. If this total is within your overall available funds, you know you have the financial resources to engage your entire PR plan. You may not yet have the personnel resources to make everything happen, but you know the funding is secure.

On the other hand, if your project budgets total exceeds your available funding, you will have to do a cost-benefit analysis to see what projects can be cut from your plan. Prioritize projects by which ones are critical to ongoing agency operations, which ones offer the most benefit to the community, and which projects offer the largest benefit for the least cost. List all the projects in descending priority order. Start cutting from the bottom until the sum of your individual project budgets fit within your available funds.

Side Bar

Example of a PR Plan's Project Description for an Ongoing Effort

* *Project:* Senior Fall Prevention
* *Targeted audiences:*
  * Retirement communities
  * Assisted living facilities
  * Skilled nursing facilities
* *Purpose:* Locations with concentrated populations of senior adults represent high risk of injuries due to inadvertent falls. Reducing the number of falls improves community health and lowers agency costs and responder risks by reducing the number of calls run.
* *Goal:* 10 percent reduction in the number of senior fall calls on an annual basis.
* *Strategies:*
  * Speaking engagements to facility residents
  * Fall prevention fair in retirement communities
  * Fall prevention training to facility staff
  * Voluntary home safety inspections
  * Balance and strength exercise programs
* *Performance and deadline benchmarks:*
  * Month 1—all facilities identified and contact information on file
  * Month 2—all facilities contacted to arrange programs
  * Months 3–6—engage strategies

* Month 7—evaluate effectiveness of efforts to date, implement changes as needed to meet year-end goal
* Months 8–11—continue efforts with changes as identified in Month 7 evaluation
* Month 12—Evaluate annual performance, draft project summary report and recommendations for the following 12-month period
* *Budget:* $5,000 for labor and materials
* *Responsible person:* Captain Kearney

ENGAGE PARTNERS

Once your PR plan is complete, distribute it to your agency's strategic partners. Give them an opportunity to help you spread information to many of the same target audiences. At the same time, if any partner has developed a PR plan of their own, see if they will share it with you. Use your plans to enlist assistance from each other at public events. (See Figure 9.1.) You and your partners may all be having the same budget and staffing shortages. Pooling your resources will increase everyone's capabilities.

Share your plan, or at least relevant parts of it, with any corporate partners. Encourage them to become project sponsors. Additional sponsorship funds can help in a number of ways. A planned event can be larger than originally envisioned. If it is a bicycle helmet giveaway, the new funds could increase the number of helmets you can purchase and hand out. Sponsor funds can help you augment your outreach efforts, whether it is to publicize a specific event, or add new strategies to an ongoing project. At the very least, a new influx of dollars may help you divert other funds and add back some projects that had been cut due to insufficient funding.

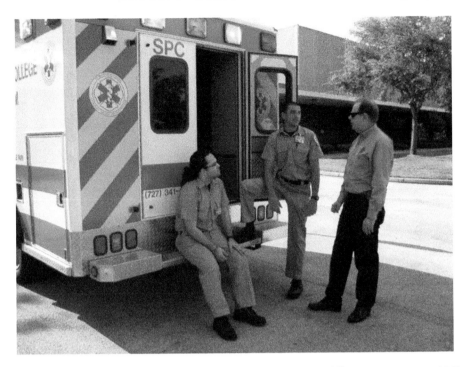

FIGURE 9.1 ▪ Use your plans to enlist assistance from each other at public events. *Courtesy of Jeffrey T. Lindsey, Ph.D.*

EMPOWER AGENCY STAFF

Any successful PR plan will require effort to implement its strategies and achieve its goals. The more assistance you can recruit, the more work can be accomplished. Enlist and empower staff throughout your agency to help inform and educate the public they are there to serve. Staff members in stations have opportunities to interact with the public over the phone, via email inquiries, and in person. (See Figure 9.2.) Responders are the public face of the agency and interact with the public on every call. Even when off the job, everyone comes in contact with people who know they are affiliated with the agency and may ask questions. Get your own agency staff informed, educated, and trained to implement your PR plan.

Internal Communications

The first internal communication with agency staff is to distribute copies of your PR plan. If it is too cumbersome or expensive to hand out printed copies to everyone, at least make copies for every station. Place an electronic copy on the agency's website in an area protected from public view. Use email blasts to solicit assistance from everyone in your agency. Refer them to the PR plan and encourage them to find an area where they would feel comfortable helping. Assure them that training and information will be available for their chosen project.

Email blasts are also an efficient means of keeping everyone informed on upcoming PR needs and current events in the agency. When press releases are sent to the media, e-blast

FIGURE 9.2 ■ Staff members in stations have opportunities to interact with the public over the phone, via email inquiries, and in person. *Courtesy of Jeffrey T. Lindsey, Ph.D.*

them to all personnel as well so they are better able to answer questions from the public who may have read the ensuing story in the local newspaper.

Once members have begun helping out with PR projects, create a non-public internal blog area on your agency's website. Agency members can use the blog to exchange experiences, suggestions, compliments, complaints, and ideas with each other. Let everyone benefit from everyone else's experiences.

Daily Briefs

Take 15 minutes during each shift or scheduled training event to promote the PR plan. (See Figure 9.3.) Offer training on how to recognize teachable moments with the public and how to use these moments to implement an informational or educational project strategy.

For example, the patient care providers are completing their tasks with the patient. One crew member is standing back, away from the action, talking with a family member. The family member comments on how kind, compassionate, and professional the caregivers are and wished he knew more about health care. This could be an opportunity to do some soft-sell recruiting for volunteers or employees, depending on your agency staffing.

If personnel who have engaged in PR activities are present, solicit feedback on their recent experiences. Use the positive accounts of their activities to spark interest in the minds of others present. Follow up the remarks with a solicitation for assistance at the next upcoming event and for ongoing projects. Pair up new recruits with experienced personnel as mentors to help train and coach them until they become comfortable with the information and methods.

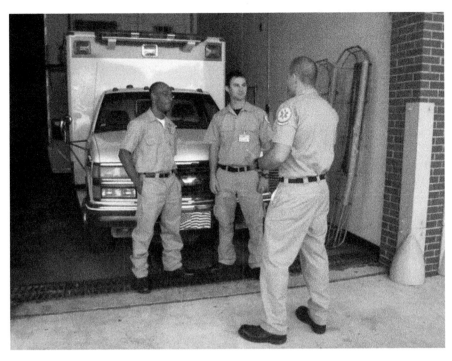

FIGURE 9.3 ▦ Take 15 minutes during each shift or scheduled training event to promote the PR plan. *Courtesy of Jeffrey T. Lindsey, Ph.D.*

Speaker's Bureau

Patient care providers are great communicators. It is a large part of doing their job. Invite them to become part of an agency **speaker's bureau**. Let each member select his or her own topic or topics that correspond to projects and priorities listed in the PR plan. Speakers may also have preferences for the types of audiences, age groups, locations, hours, or days of the week. Try to accommodate each preference in order to maximize the number of speakers available. Offer as much guidance and informational input as each requires to get their presentations prepared and practiced to the point where they are ready to be scheduled in the community.

Potential Venues   Once you have built a cadre of speakers and topics, distribute a press release announcing the formation of a speaker's bureau and how community groups can book a speaker. Send a copy of the press release to schools, neighborhood associations, political groups, service clubs, and other special-interest societies you have on file. Post a list of topics and content descriptions on your agency's website. As requests come in, match your speakers to each audience, location, topic, and time.

Training and Support   Even with experience in patient communications, EMS responders will find that public speaking is different from one-to-one contact with a patient. Certain professional standards should be followed when creating the programs each speaker will be presenting, whether it is a simple speech or an interactive computer-based program.

Just as training and practice improve patient care skills, training and practice are essential ingredients in creating an exceptional speaker. Be sure each speaker has access to classes and training materials to learn how to create and present professional programs. Make sure the content is consistent with the information and education the agency wants made public. If the speaker is creating the program, it must be approved by the agency before being presented to the public. Provide accurate and attractive handout materials that support their program. Give them a chance to practice in-house, with constructive feedback, until they feel ready to perform in public.

■ ASSESS IMPACTS

Strategies in any PR plan are only as good as the impact they have on achieving the plan's project goals. The way impacts are measured is by the use of benchmarks. Benchmarks exist to measure progress toward each project's goal. Benchmarks are met when the strategies are implemented correctly and within the designated timeframe. In this instance, the impact is positive and activities within the project move on to the next strategy on the path to meeting the project's goal.

When benchmarks are not met, strategies and actions must be assessed to see what has failed. Different methods are available to help answer assessment questions proactively and reactively.

ACTIVE OBSERVERS

Active observers can play a key role in gathering assessment data on public events. Your personnel who are actively engaged in the public event can offer some feedback, but their attention is understandably focused more on what they are doing than on the crowd. During events with widespread community participation, such as

health fairs, use retailers' secret shopper concept. Have non-uniformed people mingle at random in the crowd. Have them watch public reactions to agency personnel's actions. Are the community members engaged, moderately interested, ignoring the presentation, or seemingly bored? Listen to the audience talking among themselves to gauge their interest in the agency's presentation. Compare notes with what the presenters noticed and report back on the positives and negatives seen and heard in order to make the next event more engaging and appropriate.

Send along a second person to assist and observe at single-speaker events. The assistant can help with room setup, sign-in sheets, handout distribution, and anything else the speaker may want done in order to focus on the presentation. The assistant can monitor the crowd during the presentation for signs of rapt attention, moderate interest, sheer boredom, and all stages in between. Later, correlate the mood of the crowd with the information being presented at the time in order to improve the content of future events. Consider the questions asked and decide if that information should become part of the program for future audiences.

Public event secret shoppers and speaker's assistants will return more valuable data if they know what type of information is being sought. Provide them with a checklist that details what to look for based on what measures are being evaluated. Knowing what the desired outcomes are given them criteria by which to document and report back their observations.

ONGOING EVALUATION OF PR PLAN

Active observers can be valuable tools, but they can only cover the small number of the PR plan's strategies being utilized at that time. The way you can tell if all individual strategies are working is by periodically reviewing every benchmark throughout the plan. Once the PR plan has been approved, create a benchmarks calendar. Go through the plan, pull out every benchmark from every project, and list them in date order on a calendar. This calendar will be your reminder of what needs to be checked on an ongoing basis without your having to go through the entire plan with each periodic review.

Following are some examples of projects and benchmarks:

Project	Benchmark
CPR classes	Increase number of attendees per class 10 percent by Month 6.
	Increase number of classes held by 50 percent by Month 12.
Call 9-1-1	Increase survival rates for patients with out-of-hospital cardiac and stroke events by 5 percent by Month 12.
Call 9-1-1	Reduce average time from onset of chest pain to 9-1-1 call to under 30 minutes by Month 12.
Bike Helmets	Increase bicycle helmets distributed by 20 percent over last year during June through September.
Senior Falls	Reduction senior fall calls by 10 percent by Month 12.
Public Events	Host or participate in at least four public events every quarter.
Speaker's Bureau	Book at least one speaking engagement per week by Month 3.
	Book at least two speaking engagements per week by Month 6.
	Book at least three speaking engagements per week by Month 9.
Media References	Monthly—compile number of positive references about the agency in the media versus the total number of media references to the agency.
Recruiting	Start each biannual recruit orientation training class with at least 15 students.

When you find unmet benchmarks, start looking at possible reasons why. Was the accompanying strategy faulty or unachievable? Was the project understaffed, or staffed with ineffective personnel? Was training lacking? What internal or external forces prevented the strategy from being implemented? Was the benchmark or its timeline unrealistic? Bad strategy, bad methods, bad benchmark, or a combination of all three? Resolve the barriers and renew your quest toward achieving the affected project's goal.

REPORT TO SUPERIORS

Keep your superiors informed on the plan's progress as you monitor your PR plan's progress through ongoing evaluation and checking benchmarks. Periodically offer a written assessment with the following content:

* Planned goals versus achieved goals since the last reporting period
* What strategies and methods have worked and why
* What did not work, why, and what corrective action is being taken
* Sample materials—show them what they're paying for
* Testimonials where appropriate
* What knowledge has been gained that will improve future efforts
* What lessons have been learned that will improve future efforts
* What steps are being taken toward developing a PR plan for the next 12-month period

Once you have created a report with this content, use it as a template for future interim reports.

At the end of the 12-month plan, assemble all interim reports into a single year-end document that includes these elements:

* Executive summary of all goals that have been met
* Project-by-project synopsis of activities and achievements

- Estimated budget versus actual expenditures in total and itemized by project
- Any additional information requested by superiors
- Draft PR plan for the next 12 months, including total and per-project budgets

With this final report completed, you will be well on your way to launching a new PR plan for the following 12-month period.

CHAPTER REVIEW

Summary

Creating an information culture in your agency occurs when you empower people and give them the correct tools they need to do the job. Use teamwork to expand the reach of your public information and education outreach. Keep your team informed and educated, train them to recognize teachable moments, and focus their efforts through a written PR plan. Assess the impacts of every aspect in your PR plan: projects, strategies, methods, budgets, and people. Make changes as you go, putting more energy into what works and fixing what fails.

As each year is completed according to a written PR plan, succeeding years' plans should become easier to craft and implement. Positive results will improve support from your superiors. Recruiting and training personnel will remain an ongoing effort but should never be as difficult as the first year may have been. Veterans can become active participants in the agency's public information and education efforts. New personnel see the veterans' passion and want to join the effort. Do this, and you will have successfully created an information culture within your agency.

WHAT WOULD YOU DO? Reflection

To define and prioritize his public messaging needs, Les wrote a public relations plan. It included his informational and educational goals for the following 12 months. Some of the goals were for specific events with targeted completion dates. Other goals were ongoing projects that never end, such as fall prevention messages, bicycle helmet programs, and tips on when to call 9-1-1. For each goal, strategies for achieving the goal and potential participants from inside and outside the agency were listed. He distributed the plan to everyone within the agency and partners he had identified as potential helpers.

Once the plan had been distributed, Les started presenting different elements of the plan at shift briefings. All responders were trained to recognize teachable moments on calls and during other public interactions. Office staff were also included in order to extend the public relations reach to members of the public who call or come into the stations. As agency staff became better informed, Les began recruiting from within to create a speaker's bureau. Participants were listed according to the locations, types of message, and types of audience they were most comfortable addressing. Full support was offered to ensure each speaker had the training and professional materials needed for them to be exceptional presenters.

Review Questions

1. Name at least three public outreach strategies.
2. What are the functions of a PR plan?
3. Give at least five examples of ongoing efforts for your PR plan.
4. Give at least five examples of recurring efforts.
5. Name the components that each project or event in the plan should have clearly defined.
6. What are the cost factors you need to take into consideration for your PR plan?
7. What elements are included in a single year-end document that serves as an interim report?

References

Trevino, Mario, Lindsay White, Hendrika Meischke, and Mickey S. Eisenberg. (2008). A New Sphere for EMS. *EMS World.* See the organization website.

Yale, David R., and Andrew J. Carothers. (2001). *The Publicity Handbook, New Edition.* New York: McGraw Hill.

Key Terms

active observers Individuals attending events who are trained to watch and record actions and reactions of the audience.

public relations (PR) plan Document that contains all active public information and education projects, along with each project's audience, purpose, goal, strategies, benchmarks, budget, and responsible person.

speaker's bureau Group of experts who can make professional oral presentations to groups on request.

strategies Actions to be taken, in a specified order, to achieve a project's goals.

Glossary

active observers Individuals attending events who are trained to watch and record actions and reactions of the audience.

announcement press releases Used to distribute information to the public about routine agency business such as meetings, classes, special events, and special accomplishments.

blog A contraction of the term *web log*, where individuals post ongoing narratives written from their perspective.

boilerplate language Titles and information that do not change from one press release to the next, in particular the release date, expiration date, information contact, and agency description.

boilerplate paragraph Description of and contact information about the entity sending the press release.

brand Name, images, and perceptions developed to identify and differentiate a company, agency, or product.

breaking news Information that is deemed immediately newsworthy due to its content and timing.

capital improvement fund Money set aside to improve or build or acquire new system components with an expected usage life of more than 1 year.

criteria-based medical dispatching Sending resources to the scene of a medical emergency call based on the perceived needs as determined by comparing the caller's information to a set of standard criteria.

executive summary Brief discussion of the salient points and conclusions to be presented in detail in the report.

facilities Buildings utilized by the agency.

fact sheet Page containing authoritative data relative to a specific topic.

feature News story with an emphasis on the human-interest aspects of the topic being explored.

hard news Straightforward, fact-based description of a news event.

inverted pyramid style Type of story construction where details are presented in descending order of importance from top to bottom in the story.

language Words, sentences, and paragraphs constructed to be understood by a targeted audience.

lead A clear, concise statement that introduces the facts of the story to its readers.

macroenvironment Forces external to the organization that influence its ability to perform.

manual of style Reference document to follow for consistency in punctuation, capitalization, abbreviations, and other basic elements of writing.

marketing Organizational function and processes for creating, communicating, and delivering value to customers and for managing relationships in ways that benefit the organization.

marketing environments Forces that influence the manager's ability to attain communications objectives.

markets People or organizations with an interest in, need for, or past and present consumers of a product or service.

message Information to be communicated to an audience.

microenvironment Forces within the organization that influence the organization's ability to perform.

newsworthy Assumed to be interesting, significant, or usual enough to appeal to the general population.

noteworthy Interesting, significant, or unusual to individuals in a subset of the general population, but less broadly appealing than something that is newsworthy.

partners Persons or organizations outside the agency who help the agency do its job.

personnel Agency staff members at all levels and in all job categories, regardless of whether or not they are compensated financially for their efforts.

press releases Information sent to news media that can be used to make news or respond to news reported from another source.

public education Making a general or specific audience informed of the existence of something, along with such details as how, when, where, and why it matters to them.

public information Making a general or specific audience aware of the existence of something.

public relations plan Document that contains all active public information and education projects, along with each project's audience, purpose, goal, strategies, benchmarks, budget, and responsible person.

public relations public relations helps an organization and its publics adapt mutually to each other.

Public Safety Access Point (PSAP) Central location where calls for emergency help are received and emergency responders are dispatched.

Public Service Announcements (PSAs) Messages placed at no cost in print and electronic media for the public good.

Really Simple Syndication (RSS) Technology used to tell subscribers when information on a website has been updated.

reports Written account that formally documents a particular matter.

stakeholders Persons who control an agency's budget and rule makers who define the parameters of what patient care agency responders can do in the field.

SWOT Strengths, Weaknesses, Opportunities, and Threats.

sample A limited portion of a larger entity.

sample outlines Writing tool that allows the author to add details in order to ensure the final document is thorough and targeted properly to its audience.

SOAR Strengths, Opportunities, Aspirations, and Results.

speaker's bureau Group of experts who can make professional oral presentations to groups on request.

strategies Actions to be taken, in a specified order, to achieve a project's goals.

sunshine meetings Gatherings held by public agencies that are legally required to be open to public viewing and participation.

targeted audiences Group most likely or most desired to be receptive to communications.

targeted public groups Specific groups identified by their common needs, interests, or goals.

taxpayers Members of a community who provide funding through payment of taxes from their own personal income for public services.

testimonial Written or oral tribute.

two-tiered response system Emergency medical response system where calls are triaged by criteria-based medical dispatching into Basic Life Support (BLS) or Advanced Life Support (ALS) categories. BLS-designated calls are responded to by emergency medical technicians at Basic and Intermediate levels. ALS-designated calls are responded to by emergency medical technicians and paramedics.

writing tight copy Providing as many pertinent details as possible while simultaneously using as few words as possible.

Index

Note: Page number followed by f indicates figure.